Study Outline and Workbook in the

FUNDAMENTALS OF
MUSIC

the late
Frank W. Hill

the late
Roland Searight

revised by
Dorothy Searight Hendrickson

WCB Wm. C. Brown Publishers

Book Team
Editor *Meredith Morgan*
Developmental Editor *Susie McCormick*
Production Coordinator *Peggy Selle*
Permissions Editor *Vicki Krug*

 Wm. C. Brown Publishers

President *G. Franklin Lewis*
Vice President, Publisher *Thomas E. Doran*
Vice President, Director of Production *Beverly Kolz*
Vice President, Operations and Production *Beverly Kolz*
National Sales Manager *Virginia S. Moffat*
Marketing Manager *Kathleen Nietzke*
Executive Editor *Ed Laube*
Managing Editor, Production *Colleen A. Yonda*
Production Editorial Manager *Julie A. Kennedy*
Production Editorial Manager *Ann Fuerste*
Publishing Services Manager *Karen J. Slaght*
Manager of Visuals and Design *Faye M. Schilling*

WCB Group
President-Chief Executive Officer *Mark C. Falb*
Chairman of the Board *Wm. C. Brown*

Cover design by Sailor & Cook Creative Services
Copyedited by Siobhan Drummond

Study Outline and Workbook in the

FUNDAMENTALS OF
MUSIC

This edition of the *Study Outline and Workbook in the Elements of Music* is dedicated to the memory of Frank W. Hill and Roland Searight, and to the many students and teachers who have known the joy of learning music from the use of this book.

C O N T E N T S

P R E F A C E

A child learning to sing a song becomes involved in pitch, rhythm, melody, expression and form whether or not he or she is aware of it at the time. The young student learning to read a song is confronted with the staff, its clef signs, notes, rhythm, key signatures, and accidentals, each one important to the ultimate ability to read music. These students, who will be challenged at first by just learning the words of the song, may later become aware of the notes and the contour of the notes. Around the same time they may learn that the rhythm is marked by measures. Many will enter an adult class in music fundamentals with no more knowledge of music than these basics. Many will still be learning songs by rote. A few will have been fortunate to have had some private music instruction or some training from a parent.

At this point the teacher is challenged to find an approach suited to the needs of a wide variety of backgrounds. *Study Outline* and *Workbook* in the *Fundamentals* of *Music* has maintained an approach over the years that has been successful for many teachers.

In the fifty years of its evolvement and growth this workbook has seen the expansion of text and worksheets in the areas of notation, rhythm, scales, the keyboard, harmony, and creating music, and the addition of exercises for singing, a section on melody, a song supplement, and guitar chords. In this tenth edition an appendix on learning to play the recorder has been added for those students and teachers who may not have access to keyboards.

As the book has grown, it has become necessary as an aid to organization and planning to divide the material into chapters. Teachers should still feel free to present the material in the order of their preference.

I wish to thank the following reviewers for their helpful comments and suggestions in the preparation of this tenth edition: David Ernst, CUNY New York College and James Klausman, Edinboro University.

I wish also to thank the very supportive staff at Wm. C. Brown Publishers in Madison, Wisconsin, and Dubuque, Iowa.

Dorothy Searight Hendrickson

THE · ELEMENTS · OF · MUSIC

The Elements of Music

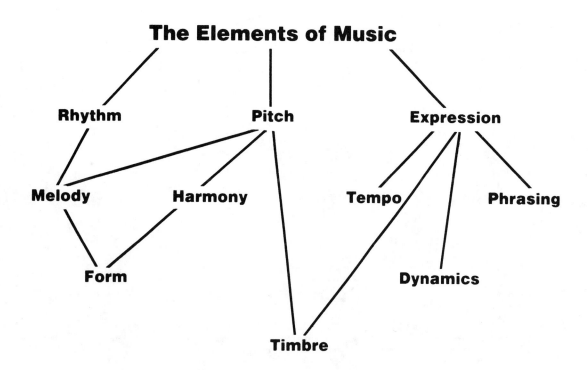

CHAPTER 1

T H E · S T A F F

To represent **pitch** (how high or low a sound is) we use a device called a **staff.** A staff consists of a series of parallel lines that might be likened to a ladder, since the higher the tone symbols are placed on the staff, the higher the pitch is. But unlike a ladder, we use the spaces between the lines, as well as the lines themselves, for steps. We call the lines and spaces of the staff **degrees.**

Eleven lines, the center one implied, compose the **great staff.** Letters are used to represent each degree on the staff. Only seven different letters—A through G—are needed to represent degrees. The eighth degree above the first uses the same letter name as the first. This series, or any series of eight degrees, is called an **octave.** The bottom line on the great staff is G and the top line is F, with the others in order as shown in the diagram. Thus, tones are named in reference to their locations on the staff.

Note that the middle line is C. Therefore, we call the tone on this line **middle C.** Unless the line is required to locate a tone, it is more convenient to omit this line. Thus, the great staff resolves into two sets of five lines each (a total of ten lines).

Middle C

To understand the degrees better, these particular staffs are placed close together. In common usage, the two five-line staffs that compose the great staff are much farther apart and are connected by a bracket (see page 5).

Due to the different voice ranges, often only one set of five lines is needed. Then it is necessary to designate by a **clef sign** which five-line staff is being used. These clef signs originally were alphabet letters, but they have changed so much through the centuries that it is difficult to see in them the letters they once represented.

For the higher staff, the **treble** or **G staff,** we use the following sign, which once was the letter G. When placed as follows,

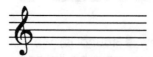

this symbol locates G on the second line from the bottom.

For the lower staff we use the following symbol:

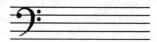

Originally, it was the letter F. When placed on the staff in the manner shown, the symbol locates F on the fourth line from the bottom and so designates the **bass** or **F staff.**

Both staffs, connected by a vertical line, are used in piano music. When middle C appears on the staff, a short line runs through the tone symbol. Similar short lines, called **ledger lines** (sometimes spelled *leger*), are used to extend the upper and lower ranges of either staff. For example, the tone located on the first ledger line above the treble staff is A, and the tone in the third space below the treble staff (which requires two ledger lines) is G. Notice that this is the same tone that would be located in the fourth space from the bottom on the bass staff.

In the following examples, you will see that each tone symbol has its own separate ledger line or lines. These lines are not connected.

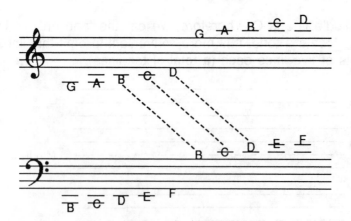

For convenience in locating a tone within a particular octave, we speak of the octave below middle C as the **small octave** and use small letters to represent the tones. The octave below the small octave is the **great octave,** and capital letters are used to represent the tones

4

in it. The next octave below is the **contra octave** with the tones indicated by double capitals, and the lowest is the **subcontra** with triple capitals used to represent its tones.

From middle C to the octave above is the **prime octave,** and the letters within this octave are written as c′, d′, and so on. The octave above the prime is the **double-prime octave,** and the letters in this octave are written as c″, d″, and so on.

The following diagram shows the most-used range of sound, covering the human voice from the lowest men's voices through high women's voices. It also covers the most-used range of the piano as well as other instruments. Notice that in this diagram each octave begins with "C." Note heads are used as symbols to specify pitch on the staff. (Notes will be explained further on page 20.)

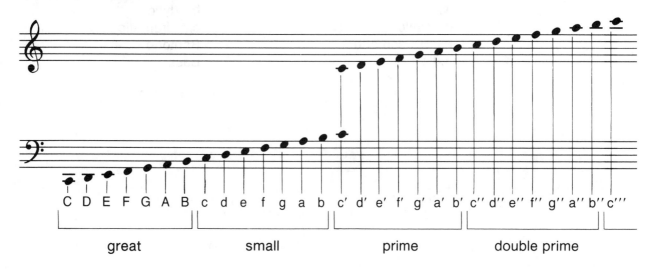

Music to be sung by a tenor voice may be designated by any one of three symbols: (1) a clef sign centered on the fourth line of the staff, which represents middle C; (2) a treble clef, with the understanding that the music will be sung an octave lower; or (3) a treble clef with the figure 8 below it to indicate that the music should be sung an octave lower.

The most common form of notation for the four-voice vocal score places the soprano and alto parts together on the treble staff and the tenor and bass parts together on the bass staff.

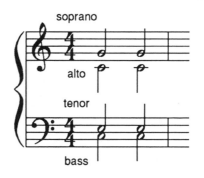

Each voice and musical instrument has its own distinctive sound quality that makes it easily recognizable. This quality is referred to as **timbre** (pronounced *tam-ber*). No two voices or instruments sound exactly alike. We use words such as *light, dark, delicate, heavy, bright, warm, smooth, shrill*, etc., in an attempt to describe these differences in timbre.

CLASSIFICATION OF SINGING VOICES

Women's Voices
1. Soprano
   a. coloratura
   b. lyric
   c. dramatic
   d. mezzo-soprano
2. Contralto

Men's Voices
1. Tenor
   a. countertenor
   b. lyric
   c. dramatic
2. Baritone
3. Bass

QUESTIONS · 1

Name _____

Date _____

1. Five horizontal lines and the spaces between them are called a _____

2. The treble staff is also called the _____

3. The bass staff is also called the _____

4. What symbol determines the letter names of the degrees on the staff? _____

5. Pitches higher or lower than the staff are indicated by _____

6. The implied line between the treble and bass staffs is called _____

7. A line or space on the staff is called a _____

8. The highness or lowness of a tone is called its _____

9. The great staff consists of how many lines? _____

10. How many tone symbols can be placed on one ledger line? _____

11. The spiral of the treble clef sign encircles what degree? _____

12. The two dots of the bass clef embrace what degree? _____

13. Each octave begins with what letter? _____

14. How far apart are C and c′′′? _____

15. What staffs are used in piano music? _____

16. How many different alphabet letters are used in music notation? _____

17. What do we call the distance from the first line to the fourth space on a staff? _____

18. What is the letter and octave name of the middle line on the treble staff? _____

19. What is the letter and octave name of the middle line on the bass staff? _____

20. What is the name of the second ledger line above the treble staff? _____

WORK · SHEET · 1

Treble and Bass Clefs, Ledger Lines

Name _____

Date _____

The treble or G clef is made with two strokes of the pen in the following manner.

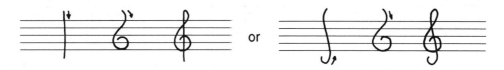

or

1. Draw treble clefs on each of the two staffs below.

2. Draw bass clefs, copying the pattern on the staff below.

3. a. On the piano staff shown below, label the following degrees with capital letters: four Gs, three Bs, four Fs, three Ds, three Es, three As. Do not use ledger lines. (Two Cs have been drawn as an example.)

    b. By means of ledger lines, locate C, G, B, and A below the treble staff.

    c. By means of ledger lines, locate A, C, D, and B above the treble staff.

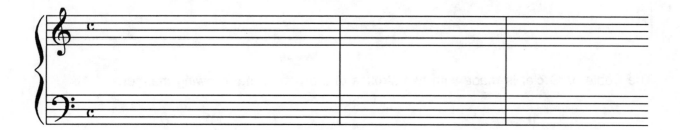

The great staff always has a bracket at the beginning. (In piano music, this usually signifies "upper staff with the right hand, lower staff with the left hand.")

WORK · SHEET · 2

Note Identification

Name _____

Date _____

Identify the note heads that appear on the staffs below. Write the letter and octave names on the lines below the staffs.

1.

_____

2.

_____

3.

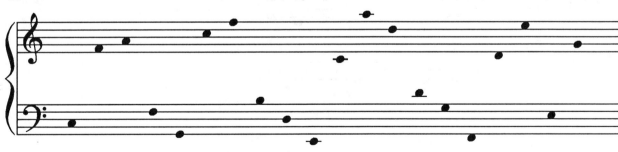

_____

4.

5.

6.

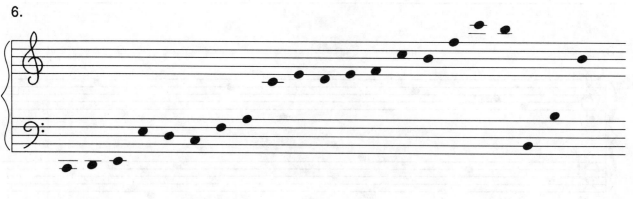

7.

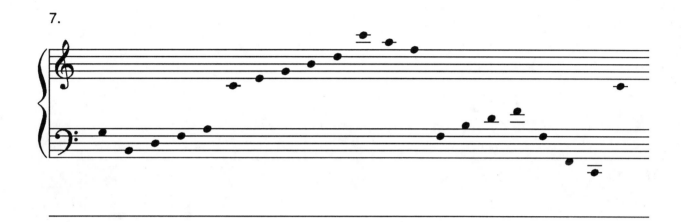

8.

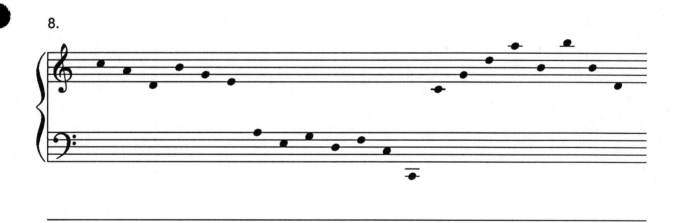

The piano keyboard is composed of white keys with black keys set at certain intervals between them. The white keys correspond to the letter names for the degrees of the staff, as shown in the diagram.

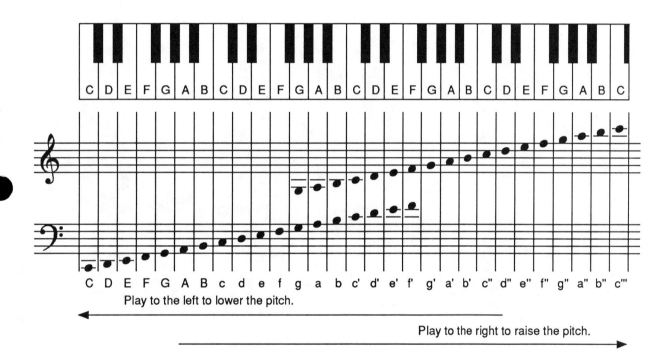

Play to the left to lower the pitch.

Play to the right to raise the pitch.

The entire keyboard on the piano contains eighty-eight keys (more than seven octaves). The four center octaves sufficiently demonstrate the relationship between the keyboard and the staff. Of course, given tones must be played in the correct octave. Therefore, we must be able to locate c′, or middle C. On the diagram above, middle C is the third C from the left since all of the keyboard is not shown. On the actual piano keyboard, middle C is the fourth C from the left (bass end of the keyboard) and is located almost in the middle of the keyboard.

The black keys are arranged in alternating groups of twos and threes to make it possible to identify the specific keys. (A solid row of black keys with a continuous row of white keys would make it very difficult to find all the Cs, Ds, and so on, without counting from the left or right of the keyboard.) To find any C on the keyboard, look for the white key immediately to the left of any group of two black keys.

WORK • SHEET • 3

Identifying Notes on the Keyboard

Name _____

Date _____

1. Middle C (c′) is given for you on the following keyboard. Write in all other Cs, giving each its proper octave designation.

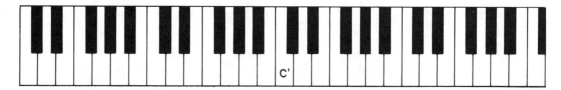

2. Write in all Ds and Gs with octave designations on the following keyboard.

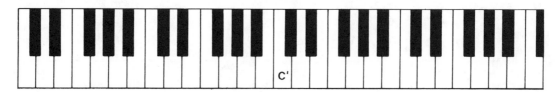

3. Write in all Fs and Bs with octave designations on the following keyboard.

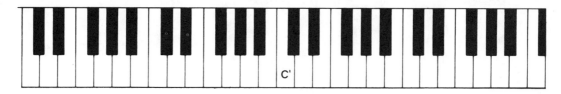

4. Write in all As and Es with octave designations on the following keyboard.

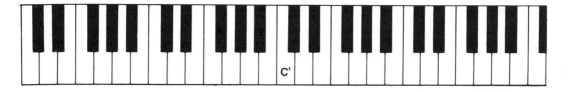

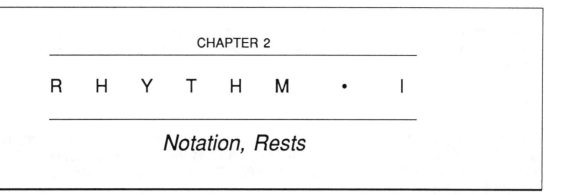

Introduction to Rhythm

Rhythm in music is a combination of **pulse** and **duration,** duration of sound and duration of silence.

The most familiar pulse is the beat of our own heart. It may beat slowly, moderately, or fast depending on the activity in which we are involved at the time. In music we refer to this rate of speed as **tempo,** meaning literally "time." For a long period in history when music was usually performed rather than written, it was left to the performer to determine the tempo. Later, after music began to be preserved in writing and printing, composers indicated the tempo in which they wished the piece to be performed by means of specific markings. Tempo indications were often combined with mood terms at the beginning of compositions. These tempo markings were written in Italian and are still used today. See Appendix 1, page 215.

The tick of a clock does not vary in speed, it marks time in determined measures of seconds, minutes, hours, days, etc. If music were to follow this exact a pattern, it would be very dull and uninteresting. It does, however, have a measure of length.

Some pulses, or beats, are stronger than others. In many compositions, the strong and weak pulses are quite easy to determine. In a flowing, gentle, or tranquil piece of music, the pulses may be so subtle that they are difficult to detect.

The following are examples of songs with strong and weak beats:

```
—  U  | —  U  | —  U  | —  U  | —  U  | —  U  | —  U | —  U
Yank - ee | Doo - dle | went  to | town  a | rid - ing | on  a | po - | ny
```

```
—  U  | —  U  | —  U  | —  U  | —  U  | —  U  | —  U
Old  Mac | Don - ald | had  a | farm, | E - I - | E - I - | O
```

```
—  U  U | —  U  U | —  U  U | —  U  U | —  U  U | —  U  U
My  coun - try | 'tis  of  thee, | sweet land of | li - ber - ty | of  thee  I | sing
```

```
—  U  U | —  U  U | —  U  U | —  U  U | —  U  U | —  U  U | —  U  U
Ca - sey would | waltz with a | straw - ber - ry | blond, And the | band | played | on
```

Duration refers to the length of sound or silence. A sound of long duration may logically have a number of feelings of pulse within it, while rapid repetitions of sound may be contained within a steady feeling of slower pulse. Sounds of various durations within a steady pulse feeling produce rhythm.

Notation

Pitches and their durations are expressed in symbols called **notes.** Different types of notes indicate that the tones they represent are sustained for different amounts of time. The placement of a note on the staff indicates its pitch. The system for showing pitch and duration (or writing music) is known as **staff notation.**

In common usage, the note of longest duration is the **whole note.** The whole note is oval and fills the space between consecutive lines of the staff.

The next note has half the duration or time value of the whole note and is called a **half note.** Its shape is like that of the whole note with the addition of a vertical line called a **stem.** If the stem points upward, it is attached to the right side of the **note head;** if the stem points downward, it goes on the left side. The length of the stem is the equivalent of three spaces. Thus, if the note head is on a line, the stem extends to the third line above or below, and if the note head is in a space, the stem extends from the middle of that space to the middle of the third space above or below. When writing single melodies on the staff, all notes on or above the middle line must have stems that point downward, and all notes below the middle line must have stems that point upward.

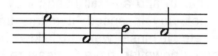

There is an exception to these rules. In a series of notes where a majority of the stems go in one direction, it is possible that a note on or above the middle line might have its stem drawn upward to conform. The same would be true of a note or notes below the middle line. See the musical examples on pages 22–23.

Four **quarter notes** combined have the duration or time value of a whole note. Quarter notes resemble half notes in shape but have solidly filled heads (see the example below). The same rules regarding stems on half notes apply to all other notes with stems.

All notes with time values less than that of a quarter note make use of **flags** attached to their stems, and the number of flags determine the note's value. The **eighth** note (one whole note is equal to eight eighths) has one flag; the sixteenth note (one whole note is equal to sixteen sixteenths) has two flags; the thirty-second note has three flags; and the sixty-fourth note has four. Flags are always placed to the right of the stem regardless of whether the stem goes up or down.

In instrumental music, notes with flags are generally joined together to give the notes "flags in common" or **beams.** This does not affect the value of the notes, but clarifies the pulse and facilitates the reading of rapid passages:

Table of Note Equivalents
Symbols of Sound

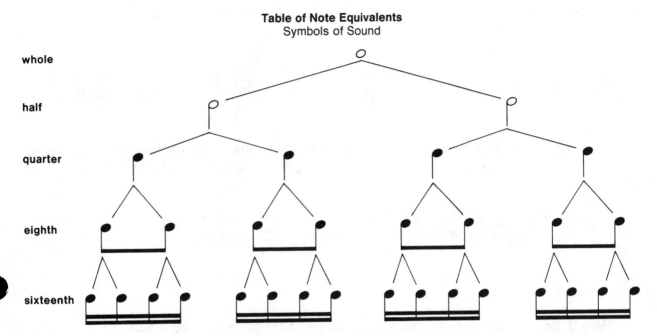

whole

half

quarter

eighth

sixteenth

In vocal music, another meaning is attached to the use of flags in common or beams. Separate flags are used, regardless of rhythmic grouping, for each note associated with a separate word syllable or vowel sound. Flags in common indicate then that the grouped notes should be sung on a common vowel. In the following example, the words *with, eyes,* and *I* each have two notes to sing with one vowel sound.*

Drink to me on - ly   with__thine eyes__ And   I____ will pledge with   mine.____

When two or more notes of the same pitch and in the same voice are connected by a curved line, the tone is sounded continuously for the combined duration of the connected notes. The curved line used in this way is known as a **tie.** (See example above on the word *mine.*)

When we wish to prolong a note by half its value, instead of tying another note to it, we often use a **dot.** A dot is equal to half the note that precedes it and adds that much to the

*It is important to note that today many publishers, particularly in the printing of popular songs, folk songs, and school music books, use all beams rather than separate flags for vocal music.

total duration. When the dot is used with a note on a line, the dot is always placed in the space above that line. Care must be exercised that dots are correctly placed because their significance may vary in other positions.

A second dot adds half the value of the first dot to the duration of the note. In other words, the second dot adds one-fourth of the note's value to the total duration.

When a series of notes with different pitches shares the same continuous vowel sound throughout the combined note values, a curved line called a **slur** connects the notes.

A migh-ty for-tress is our God, a bul-wark nev-er fail - - ing;

Here is an example of three measures plus one note connected by a slur:

Glo - ri - a

Occasionally, it is desirable to fill a time unit with an odd number of tones of equal length. The most common example of this device is the **triplet** group. In triplet groups, three notes sound in the time of two of the same value. The following melodies illustrate the use of the triplet:

"Lass with the Delicate Air"

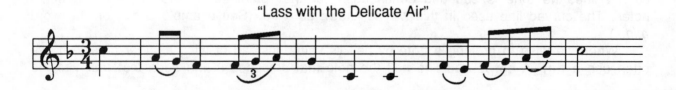

22

"Juanita"

"Once to Every Man and Nation"

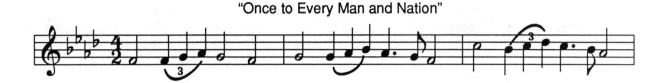

"Oh, Marie"

Since there are no note symbols for cases when the pulse is divided between an odd number of tones of equal length, notes of the value closest to that desired are used. The number of notes in the group appears above or below the notes themselves, and a curved line is often placed outside the number, its ends extending to include the group's end notes.

Duplets are two notes used in the time of three of the same value:

Duplets occur only in compound meter, which will be discussed in the next section.

Rests

The duration of silence is expressed by symbols called **rests.** For each note value, there is a corresponding rest value. The **whole rest** is a short, thick line or horizontal bar and is generally suspended from the fourth line of the staff. (If a whole rest appears outside the staff, it is suspended from a line slightly longer than the rest itself.) The **half rest** is similar to the whole rest but sits above the line instead of below it. On the staff, the half rest is generally attached to the third line. A complete table of rests follows:

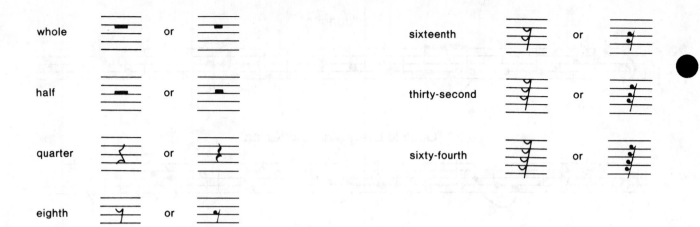

whole	or	sixteenth	or
half	or	thirty-second	or
quarter	or	sixty-fourth	or
eighth	or		

Table of Rest Equivalants
Symbols of Silence

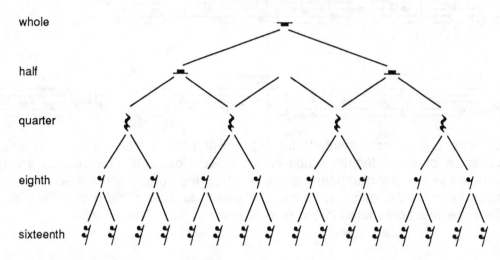

whole

half

quarter

eighth

sixteenth

Dots are sometimes added to rests. Whether note or rest, the dot is equal to half the unit that precedes it and adds that much to the total duration.

24

QUESTIONS · 2

Name _____

Date _____

1. A note placed on the staff expresses what two characteristics of a tone? _____

   _____

2. How does a half note differ in appearance from a whole note? _____

3. How does a quarter note differ in appearance from a half note?

   _____

4. What note values require the addition of a flag or flags? _____

5. Flags in common are also called _____

6. By what device can we increase the value of a single note? _____

7. The system for writing music is called _____

8. How are flags in common used in vocal music? _____

9. A half note is equal to how many eighth notes? _____

   Sixteenth notes? _____ Thirty-second notes? _____

10. How are periods of silence indicated? _____

11. A dotted half note is equal in value to how many eighth notes? _____

12. Where on the staff is a whole rest placed? _____

13. Where on the staff is a half rest placed? _____

14. What are triplets? _____

15. What is a tie? _____

16. In which direction do stems of notes above the middle line of a staff point? _____

17. In which direction do stems of notes below the middle line of a staff point? _____

18. What single rest would replace two dotted quarter notes? _____

19. A double dotted quarter note is equal to how many sixteenth notes? _____

20. On which side of note stems are flags always placed? _____

WORK · SHEET · 4

Writing Music Notes

Name _____

Date _____

To ensure uniformity in size and shape, the whole note is formed with two strokes of the pen, both from left to right. On an imaginary axis, one stroke goes over and one under, as shown in the following example:

Notice that the whole note (as with the heads of all other notes) does not lie squarely on the line but is slanted upward.

1. On the following staff, draw whole notes in all the spaces where they are crossed by diagonal lines (refer to the samples). Make the top stroke first.

2. Without the help of guidelines, fill these spaces with whole notes. Notes should be uniformly spaced.

3. Draw whole notes on the lines of the staff where they are crossed by diagonal lines.

4. Without the aid of guidelines, fill the lines of this staff with whole notes.

5. Add stems to the note heads on the staffs below.

For best results in making solidly filled heads, begin drawing at the center of the head and spread outward to the correct size, as in this sample, rather than outlining the note and then filling it in.

6. Write quarter notes alternately in the first and fourth spaces. Place the notes evenly and make stems of the correct lengths.

7. Write eighth notes on the first, middle, and fifth lines.

8. Write half notes on the first, middle, and fifth lines.

WORK · SHEET · 5

Writing Music Rests

Name _____

Date _____

The whole and half rests are probably the easiest to draw. Start with a small rectangle on or under the line and then fill in.

1. On the following staff, draw eight whole rests.

2. On the following staff, draw eight half rests.

The quarter rest is the most difficult to draw. It may be made in two ways. It may be thought of as a slightly extended and curved backward Z

⊆   to   ⟩

or as a small extended Z with a tipped c on the bottom.

⟨   to   ⟩

3. In approximately the middle of the staff, draw eight quarter rests.

The eighth rest resembles the number 7.

7 to 𝄾

It may also be started with a dot.

· to ᵕ to 𝄾

4. In approximately the middle of the staff, draw eight eighth rests.

The sixteenth, thirty-second and sixty-fourth rests are made like a stacked eighth.

᷉ to 𝄾 or ᷉ to 𝄾

5. Keeping them within the staff, draw eight sixteenth rests.

1. Write a half note and two quarter notes on each degree of the staff.

2. On this staff, make rests of the values indicated below. (One rest to the value of each fraction.)

$\frac{1}{8}$ $\frac{1}{1}$ $\frac{1}{4}$ $\frac{1}{16}$ $\frac{1}{64}$ $\frac{1}{4}$ $\frac{1}{1}$ $\frac{1}{32}$ $\frac{3}{8}$ $\frac{1}{2}$ $\frac{1}{4}$ $\frac{1}{8}$ $\frac{3}{16}$ $\frac{1}{32}$ $\frac{1}{16}$ $\frac{3}{4}$ $\frac{1}{1}$ $\frac{1}{4}$ $\frac{1}{2}$

On these staffs, write notes in the pitch and value given below. Where no pitch is given, use rests.

3.

a'	d"		c'	g'	g"	f"	b'		d'	a'	f'	c"	b'	b"		d"	c"	a'	e'
$\frac{1}{4}$	$\frac{1}{16}$	$\frac{1}{8}$	$\frac{1}{1}$	$\frac{1}{64}$	$\frac{1}{32}$	$\frac{1}{2}$	$\frac{1}{8}$	$\frac{1}{2}$	$\frac{1}{4}$	$\frac{1}{16}$	$\frac{1}{1}$	$\frac{1}{32}$	$\frac{1}{8}$	$\frac{1}{2}$	$\frac{1}{4}$	$\frac{1}{16}$	$\frac{1}{4}$	$\frac{1}{32}$	$\frac{1}{8}$

4.

A	c	e	g	b	d'		G	B	E	f	d		A	a	g	G	f	B	c
$\frac{1}{16}$	$\frac{1}{2}$	$\frac{1}{32}$	$\frac{1}{1}$	$\frac{1}{64}$	$\frac{1}{16}$	$\frac{1}{16}$	$\frac{1}{2}$	$\frac{1}{1}$	$\frac{1}{8}$	$\frac{1}{1}$	$\frac{1}{16}$	$\frac{1}{2}$	$\frac{1}{4}$	$\frac{1}{8}$	$\frac{1}{1}$	$\frac{1}{16}$	$\frac{1}{4}$	$\frac{1}{32}$	$\frac{1}{2}$

5.

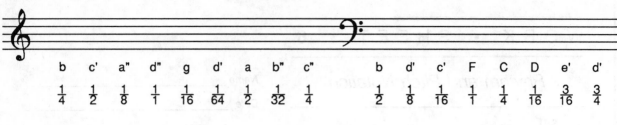

	b	c'	a"	d"	g	d'	a	b"	c"		b	d'	c'	F	C	D	e'	d'
	$\frac{1}{4}$	$\frac{1}{2}$	$\frac{1}{8}$	$\frac{1}{1}$	$\frac{1}{16}$	$\frac{1}{64}$	$\frac{1}{2}$	$\frac{1}{32}$	$\frac{1}{4}$		$\frac{1}{2}$	$\frac{1}{8}$	$\frac{1}{16}$	$\frac{1}{1}$	$\frac{1}{4}$	$\frac{1}{16}$	$\frac{3}{16}$	$\frac{3}{4}$

R H Y T H M · I I

Measure Structure, Types of Rhythm, Repeat Indicators

Measure Structure

As we have learned, in the music pulse or **beat,** some pulses are stronger than others. Since these strong pulses tend to recur regularly, they divide **melody** into small groups of tones, each group containing the same number of pulses. A melody is a series of tones sounded in rhythm or as a musical line on the staff. Melody is explained further on pages 191–192.

These groups of tones known as **measures** are separated from each other in written music by vertical lines called **bars** that run through the staff. The bar always comes before the strong pulse, which is why some melodies begin with fractional measures. If a fractional measure contains only a single beat or a fraction of one, we refer to the beat as the **anacrusis,** commonly called **upbeat** or **pickup.** (See Work Sheet 11, numbers 2, 5, and 6.) This fractional measure is subtracted from the final measure, making the final measure fractional, too. A **double bar** indicates the conclusion of the composition or of a musical unit complete in itself. The double bar can also be used in the middle of a composition to indicate a time change, key change, or separation between verse and chorus. In such cases, the double bar lines are equal. At the end of a composition, however, the double bar has a thicker second line.

As a general rule, all of the measures within a complete unit tend to contain the same number of pulses or beats. As a result, measures are said to have a certain **meter** or **time.** To indicate the time or measure content, two numbers appear as a simple arithmetic fraction at the beginning of the first measure in a piece of music. These numbers, known as **time signatures,** are not separated by a line as in a true arithmetical fraction, but the top number fills the upper two spaces of the staff and the bottom number fills the lower two spaces. The top number indicates the meter, or number of pulses per measure, and the bottom number shows the note value of each pulse. The time signature is placed on the first staff at the beginning of a composition.

There are three different types of meter: **simple, compound,** and **asymmetrical.** In simple meters each beat of a measure is divisible by two. That is to say, the **rhythmic unit** (the note value of the beat) can be represented by two of the next smaller notes and so on down to the smallest usable division. The simple meters include: **duple, triple,** and **quadruple.**

In duple time, each measure contains one strong pulse and one weak pulse:

STRONG	weak		STRONG	weak		STRONG	weak		STRONG	weak
(S)	(w)		(S)	(w)		(S)	(w)		(S)	(w)

This compares to trochaic meter in poetry:

Love   some-   bod   - y;   yes   I   do!

Simple Duple Meters

$\frac{2}{2}$ (or $\frac{2}{\text{half note}}$) ← a half note is the rhythmic unit

Often the $\frac{2}{2}$ time signature is written with the sign $\mathbf{\mathrm{C\!\!\!|}}$ commonly called "cut time.",

Gruber

O - ver hill, o - ver dale, we have hit the dus - ty trail, As those cais - sons go roll - ing a - long.

$\frac{2}{4}$ (or $\frac{2}{\text{quarter note}}$) ← a quarter note is the rhythmic unit

$\frac{2}{8}$ (or $\frac{2}{\text{eighth note}}$) ← an eighth note is the rhythmic unit

Source: Leon Dallin and Lynn Dallin, *Heritage Songster,* 2d ed. Copyright © 1980 Wm. C. Brown Publishers, Dubuque, Iowa. All Rights Reserved.

An example of a song in simple duple time:

For the complete song, see page 222 in the Song Supplement section.

In triple time, each measure contains one strong pulse and two weaker pulses:

STRONG weak weak | STRONG weak weak | STRONG weak weak
(S)   (w) (w) | (S)   (w) (w) | (S)   (w) (w)

The poetry meter is dactylic:

Down yŏn - dĕr grĕen vāl - lĕy whĕre strēam - lĕts mĕ - āndĕr

Simple Triple Meters

$\frac{3}{2}$ (or $\frac{3}{2}$) ← a half note is the rhythmic unit

$\frac{3}{4}$ (or $\frac{3}{4}$) ← a quarter note is the rhythmic unit

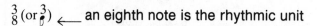
$\frac{3}{8}$ (or $\frac{3}{\text{♪}}$) ← an eighth note is the rhythmic unit

S w w S w w S w w
1 2 3 1 2 3 1 2 3

An example of a song in simple triple time:

"The Ash Grove"

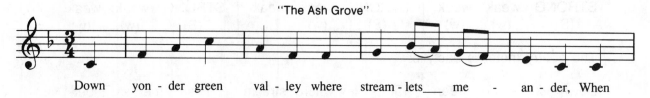

Down   yon - der green   val - ley where   stream - lets___ me - an - der, When

For the complete song, see page 219 in the Song Supplement section.

In quadruple time, each measure contains one strong pulse and three weaker pulses. The third pulse is slightly stronger than the second and fourth pulses:

| STRONGEST | weak | strong | weak | STRONGEST | weak | strong | weak | STRONGEST | weak | strong | weak |
| (S) | (w) | (s) | (w) | (S) | (w) | (s) | (w) | (S) | (w) | (s) | (w) |

The poetry meter, trochaic, is the same as for duple time (see page 33).

Simple Quadruple Meters

$\frac{4}{2}$ (or $\frac{4}{\text{♩}}$) ← a half note is the rhythmic unit

Plus two more groups
of eighth notes

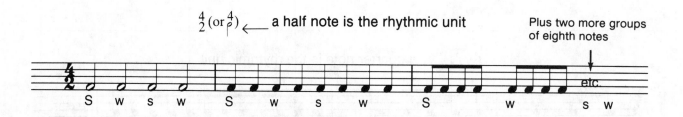

S w s w S w s w S w s w

In $\frac{4}{2}$ time, you will notice that a measure may contain four half notes. You have also learned that two half notes equal one whole note. Therefore, $\frac{4}{2}$ time may make use of the double whole note: ▭. This was commonly used in church music of the fifteenth through eighteenth centuries but is not commonly used today. However, it is still seen in some hymnals

36

and is used in some contemporary compositions such as Samuel Barber's "Adagio for Strings" and "Christmas Cantata for Chorus and Double Brass Choir" by Daniel Pinkham.

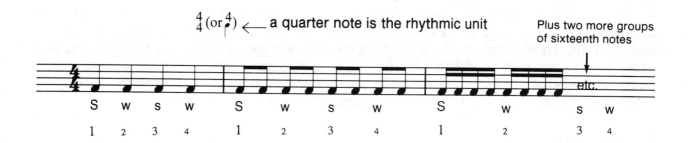

Often the $\frac{4}{4}$ time signature is written with the sign, referred to as "common time."

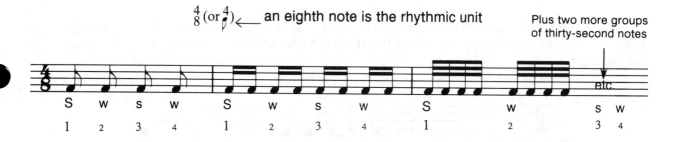

An example of a song in simple quadruple time:

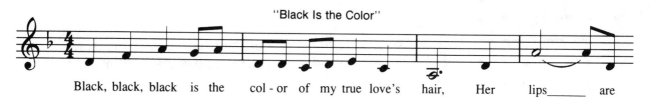

"Black Is the Color"

Black, black, black is the col - or of my true love's hair, Her lips_____ are

For the complete song, see page 228 in the Song Supplement section.

In duple time, if we wish to divide the beat consistently into three parts, the total value for each beat equals that of a dotted quarter note:

Since there is no number to substitute for the value of a dotted quarter note and the measure now contains six beats, each an eighth note, we can make the time signature $\frac{6}{8}$. Thus, $\frac{6}{8}$ is **compound duple meter;** that is, a combining of six beats within two main beats, or duple meter with each beat divided into three parts equal in value. The other compound meters are **compound triple** and **compound quadruple.**

In compound meter, the top number of the time signature represents the number of pulses for each measure, as it did in simple meter. However, because each pulse is divided into three, the upper number will always be a multiple of three. It is also important to note that even though each pulse is divided into three and each pulse is counted, there are still strong pulses and weaker pulses as there were in simple meter. Therefore, the bottom number of the time signature, representing the strongest pulses, results in a dotted note.

Compound Duple Meter

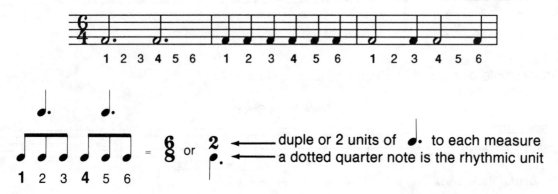

Each measure must contain six quarter notes or any combination of notes equal to six quarter notes, provided they are within the rhythmic unit and do not change the basic pulse of the measure.

Each measure must contain six eighth notes or any combination of notes equal to six eighth notes, provided they are within the rhythmic unit and do not change the basic pulse of the measure.

An example of a song in compound duple time:

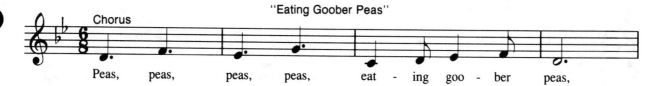

Compound Triple Meter

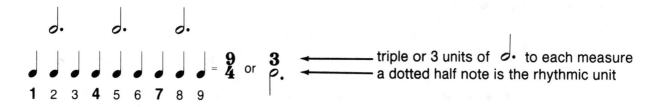

triple or 3 units of 𝅗𝅥. to each measure
a dotted half note is the rhythmic unit

Each measure must contain nine quarter notes or any combination of notes equal to nine quarter notes.

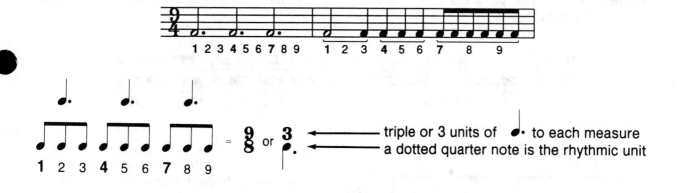

triple or 3 units of ♩. to each measure
a dotted quarter note is the rhythmic unit

Each measure must contain nine eighth notes or any combination of notes equal to nine eighth notes.

An example of a song in compound triple time:

"Morning Has Broken"

Morn - ing has bro - ken   Like the first   morn - ing   Black-bird has   spo - ken   Like the first

For the complete song, see page 223 in the Song Supplement section.

Compound Quadruple Meter

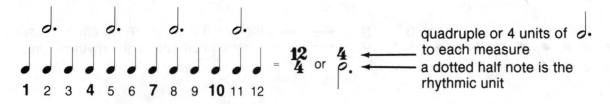

quadruple or 4 units of 𝅗𝅥. to each measure
a dotted half note is the rhythmic unit

Each measure must contain twelve quarter notes or any combination of notes equal to twelve quarter notes, provided they are within the rhythmic unit and do not change the basic pulse of the measure.

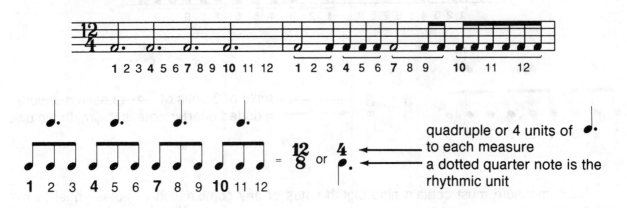

quadruple or 4 units of ♩. to each measure
a dotted quarter note is the rhythmic unit

Each measure must contain twelve eighth notes or any combination of notes equal to twelve eighth notes, provided they are within the rhythmic unit and do not change the basic pulse of the measure.

An example of a song in compound quadruple time:

"He Shall Feed His Flock Like a Shepherd"

from Handel's *Messiah*

Compare measures of $\frac{3}{2}$ and $\frac{6}{4}$ or of $\frac{3}{4}$ and $\frac{6}{8}$. The notes must be grouped differently, even though the duration of the measure is identical.

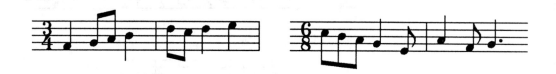

If a composition contains a deliberate shift in rhythm from three pulses to two pulses or from two pulses to three pulses, the alteration is known as a **hemiola.**

Catherine Winkworth, translator

"Comfort, Comfort Ye My People"

Genevan Psalter 1551

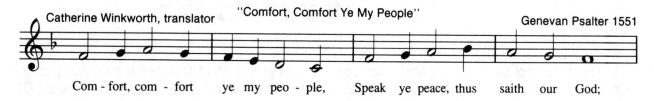

Com - fort, com - fort   ye my peo - ple,   Speak ye peace, thus   saith   our   God;

Aaron Copland
Fourth theme

El Salón Mexico (for orchestra)

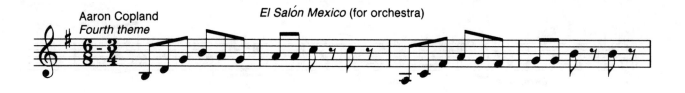

Asymmetrical Meter

The third type of meter, asymmetrical meter, is obtained by combining dissimilar simple meters. Thus, five-pulse meter is a combination of duple and triple meter, and seven-pulse meter is a combination of triple and quadruple meter.

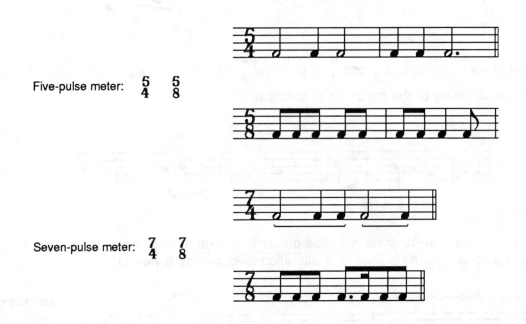

Five-pulse meter: $\frac{5}{4}$ $\frac{5}{8}$

Seven-pulse meter: $\frac{7}{4}$ $\frac{7}{8}$

The following example is from a composition by the late Paul Desmond, alto saxophonist with the Dave Brubeck Quartet, a contemporary jazz group (recorded by Columbia Records CL 2484, Stereo 9284). The composition is called "Take Five" and is in the difficult $\frac{5}{4}$ meter.

Good examples of unusual meter may be found in Aaron Copland's *El Salón Mexico and* Béla Bartók's *Mikrokosmos* for piano, volume VI.

Types of Rhythm

Rhythm is the pattern of distribution of note values in a measure. When the note values are uniformly distributed among the beats or pulses in a measure, the rhythm is **uniform**. When the longer notes in a measure occur on the strong pulse, the rhythm is **regular,** and when the shorter notes fall on the strong pulse, the rhythm is said to be **irregular.** Finally, when the longer notes in a measure occur on unaccented fractions of pulses, the rhythm is **syncopated.** In syncopated rhythm, we always find a note or rest of less value than a beat, followed by a note of greater value (which is usually given emphasis).

The vertical lines indicate the beats.

An example of syncopated and irregular rhythms:

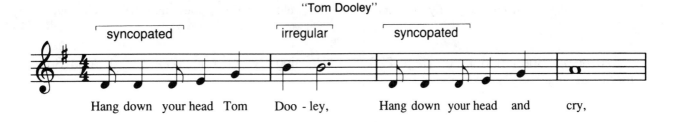

43

Repeat Indicators

Dots in the second and third spaces of the staff and to the left of a double bar indicate that the section ending there is to be repeated. If a section in the middle of a piece of music is to be repeated, dots are also placed to the right of the double bar just before the part that is to be repeated, and only that section is performed a second time. Sometimes a repeated section does not end in exactly the same way the first and second times. In this case, a line is drawn over the top of the first ending measure or measures with a number "1" to mark it, and the second ending follows the repeat bar and is marked with a line and number "2" over it. In sounding the section for the second time, the first ending is omitted and the second one is performed instead.

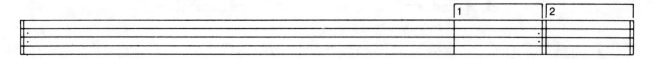

The letters **D.C.,** which are sometimes found over the final measure of a composition, are an abbreviation for the words **da capo,** which means to repeat from the beginning. **D.S. (dal segno)** is an indication to repeat from the sign%. After either a D.C. or a D.S., the word **fine** is used to mark the end of the piece.

When a single tone or rest is to be sustained beyond its written value, a **fermata** or pause mark is placed over or under the note or rest: ⌢ The duration of such pauses or holds is indefinite and is governed by the music judgment of the performer. A fermata over a double bar indicates that there will be a prolongation between sections.

An example of fermata:

"The Man on the Flying Trapeze"

See also, "Shenandoah" on page 220 and "Passing By" on page 222 in the Song Supplement section.

Q U E S T I O N S · 3

Name _____

Date _____

1. Portions of equal duration on the staff are called _____

2. The conclusion of a composition or section is indicated by _____

3. The time or measure content of a composition is indicated by _____

4. What are the different types of meter? _____

5. What are the different types of simple meters? _____

6. How many strong pulses are found in each measure of simple meter? _____

7. What kind of note constitutes the rhythmic unit in compound meter? _____

8. What single note is equal to three eighth notes? _____

9. What device indicates a section is to be repeated? _____

10. What do the letters D.C. mean? _____

11. What do the letters D.S. mean? _____

12. What is meant by the word *fine?* _____

13. What is a fermata? _____

14. When the longer notes occur on unaccented fractions of beats, the rhythm is of what

type? _____

15. What single rest is equal to three quarter rests? _____

16. Six-pulse is a compound of what simple meter? _____

17. Nine-pulse is a compound of what simple meter? _____

18. Twelve-pulse is a compound of what simple meter? _____

19. What are two examples of combined or asymmetric meter? _____

20. What is a rhythmic unit? _____

Identification of Measures

Name _____

Date _____

1. Place bar lines in the proper places, assuming each staff begins on the first count.

a.

b.

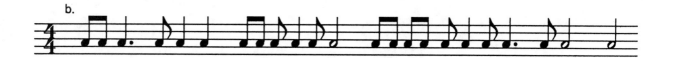

c.

2. Add *one* note to each measure below to complete the meter.

a.

b.

3. Put in the proper time signature for each of the following measures.

WORK · SHEET · 8

Identifying Measures with Rests

Name _____

Date _____

1. Assuming each staff begins on the first count, place bar lines in the proper places.

a.

b.

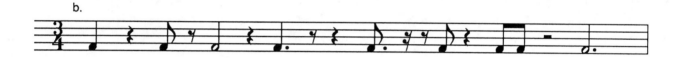

c.

2. Add *one* rest to each measure below to complete the meter.

a.

b.

50

WORK · SHEET · 9

Rhythm and Pitch Notation

Name _____

Date _____

In these exercises, write the note indicated by the letter and figure below the staff. Where there are no letters, use rests. When you have put all of the notes and rests in, go back and put in the bars. Both $\frac{3}{8}$ and $\frac{3}{16}$ refer to dotted notes.

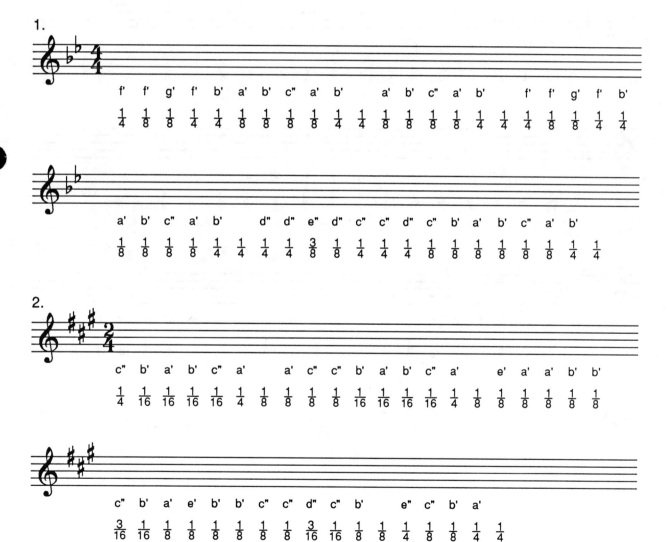

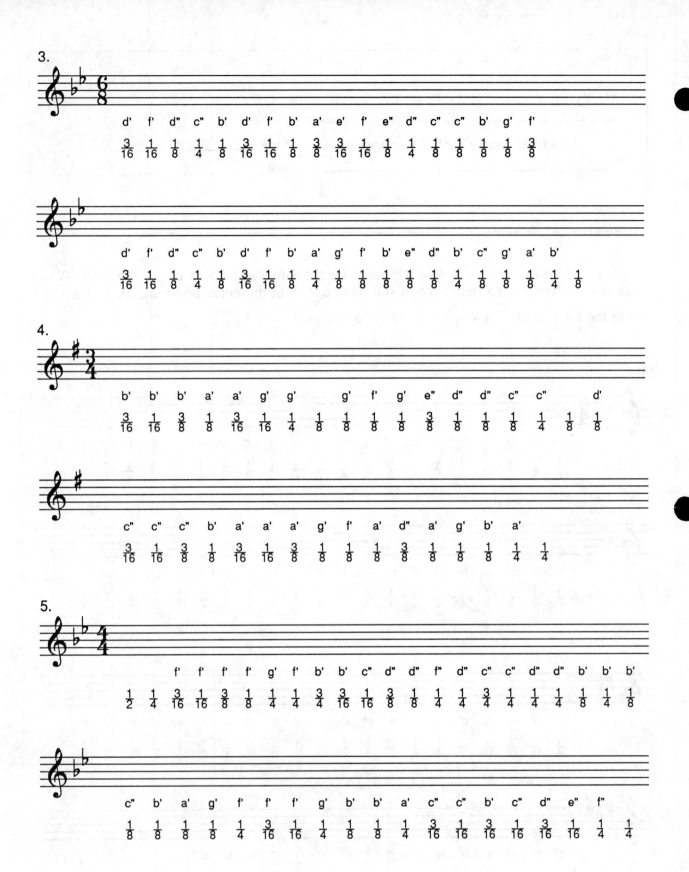

52

Name _____

Date _____

6.

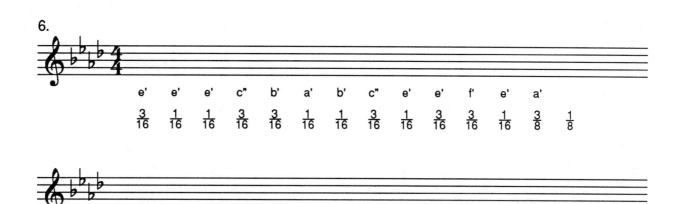

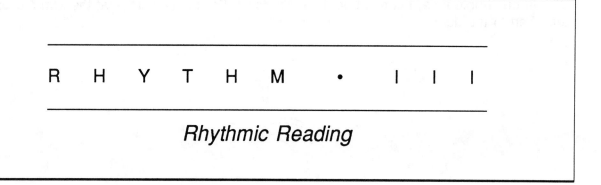

R H Y T H M · I I I

Rhythmic Reading

Ways to Read Rhythms

There are two basic ways to read rhythm aloud:
1. Count the meter aloud ("1-2" in a two-beat measure; "1-2-3" in a three-beat measure; and so on). Clap the notated rhythm as you count.
2. Clap the meter or use the conductor's beat pattern and read the notated rhythm in rhythmic syllables.

Conducting Patterns

In order for the performers to conform to the same rhythmic beat and tempo, larger groups of instruments or singers have a leader, referred to as a conductor. Using the right hand or a baton, conductors indicate these beats with basic patterns, varied somewhat by individual style.

The first beat of the measure is referred to as the *downbeat* and is made with a downward motion of the arm. In duple time, the second beat is the weaker beat and is indicated by an upward motion:

In triple time the first beat, the strong beat, is once again made with a strong downward motion. The second beat, a weak beat, is a motion to the right, and beat three, also a weak beat, is the upward return:

In quadruple time, the first beat is again down. For the second beat the arm moves to the left, then to the right for three and up for four:

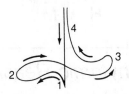

A diagram for $\frac{6}{8}$ time would look like this:

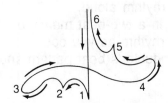

For a fast tempo in $\frac{6}{8}$ time, the pattern for simple duple would be used.

In order for the beat to be determined easily by those observing, the conducting patterns should be neither too rigid and mechanical nor executed with too much flourish.

Practice each pattern, keeping the beat constant, until the pattern becomes automatic. Count the meter aloud, or sing a familiar song in the appropriate meter as you practice.

Rhythmic Syllables

This well-known system for reading rhythm makes use of easily pronounced syllables. The following examples of four-beat measures demonstrate the use of these syllables.

1. When each beat is divided into two equal parts, the syllables *one-and, two-and, three-and, four-and* are used to count the rhythm.

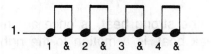

Clap the beat or use the four-beat conductor's pattern and read the following patterns. Use only those syllables indicated by the notes in the rhythm pattern. Repeat each line until the correct syllables become automatic.

56

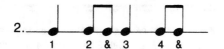

2.
1   2 & 3   4 &

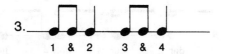

3.
1 & 2   3 & 4

4.
1 &   & 3 &   &

5.
1   & 3   &

2. When each beat is divided into four equal parts, the syllables *one-a-and-a, two-a-and-a* (pronounced *one-a-an-duh, two-a-an-duh*) and so on are used to count the rhythm.

1.
1 a an duh 2 a an duh 3 a an duh 4 a an duh

Clap the beat or use the four-beat conductor's pattern and read the following patterns. Use only those syllables indicated by the notes in the rhythm pattern. Repeat each line until the correct syllables become automatic.

2.
1   an duh 2   an duh 3   an duh 4   an duh

3.
1 a an 2 a an 3 a an 4 a an

4. | 1 a duh 2 a duh 3 a duh 4 a duh

5. | 1 duh 2 duh 3 duh 4 duh

6. | 1 duh 3 duh

All simple meters of two-beat, three-beat, or slow six-beat measures use the same syllables.

Examples of rhythmic syllables set to known melodies:

58

3. Compound meters, such as $\frac{6}{8}$, $\frac{9}{8}$, $\frac{12}{8}$ in which the beats are divided into three equal parts, use the syllables *one-la-lee, two-la-lee,* and so on. If the beats are divided into six equal parts, the syllables *one-ta-la-ta-lee-ta,* and so on, are used. Practice each of these patterns until the syllables become automatic.

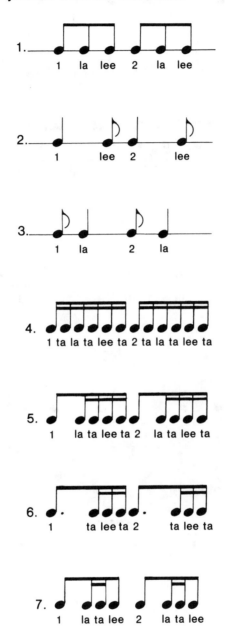

Another method of rhythmic reading was developed in the early 1900s by Hungarian composer Zoltán Kodály. The Kodály Method, based on the use of authentic folk music, was designed to teach music skills to Hungarians from nursery school years to adulthood. This method is also used in American schools and in other countries.

The following are the basic rhythm duration syllables of the Kodály Method.

ta   ti - ti   ti - ri - ti - ri   tri - o - la   syn - co - pa
(ti - ta - ti)

Simple duple:

ta   ta   ti - ti   ti - ti   ti - ri - ti - ri   ti - ri - ti - ri   ti - ti - ri   ti - ri - ti

Simple quadruple:

ta ta ta ta   ta ___ ta ___ = ta - a ta - a   ta - a - a - a = ta - a - a - a

Simple triple:

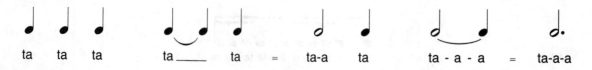

ta   ta   ta   ta ___ ta   = ta-a   ta   ta - a - a   = ta-a-a

Developing the dotted quarter note:

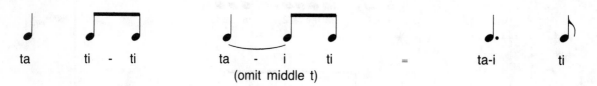

ta   ti - ti   ta - i   ti   =   ta-i   ti
(omit middle t)

Syncopation:

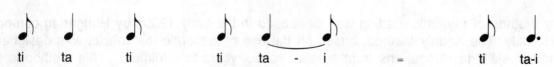

ti   ta   ti   ti   ta - i   =   ti   ta-i

Developing the dotted eighth followed by the sixteenth note:

Developing the sixteenth followed by the dotted eighth note:

A song using the Kodály syllables:

2. Old Joe Clark had a house twenty stories high,
   And every story in that house was filled with chicken pie.

WORK · SHEET · 10

Rhythmic Reading

Name _____

Date _____

Read the following rhythmic patterns using either of the two basic methods given on page 55 for reading rhythm aloud. Repeat each exercise several times. If desired, the rhythmic syllables and numbers may be written under the notes.

7.

8.

9.

10.

11.

Rhythmic Reading—Familiar Songs

Name _____

Date _____

Reading the following rhythmic patterns, using either of the two basic methods given on page 55 for reading rhythm aloud. Repeat each exercise several times. Identify the name of the song.

1.

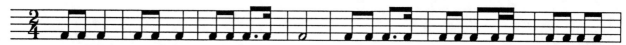

2.

3.

4.

5.

6.

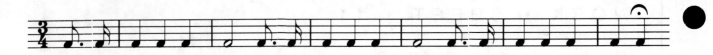

7.

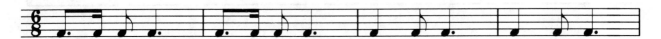

Creating Rhythms

Name _____

Date _____

Divide the following staffs into six measures each and write a different rhythmic pattern in each measure, making sure the rhythms fit the time signatures. Do not use note values smaller than an eighth and do not use rests. Place all notes on the first space. When you have completed the rhythmic patterns, read them aloud.

1.

$\frac{3}{4}$

2.

$\frac{2}{4}$

3.

$\frac{4}{4}$

4.

$\frac{6}{8}$

5.

$\frac{9}{8}$

Staves for practice writing:

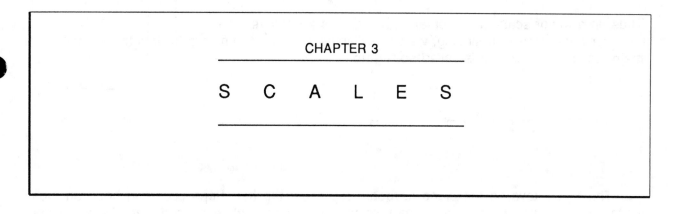

CHAPTER 3

S C A L E S

Music is composed of sounds called tones, which are produced by regular, continuous vibrations. The rate of vibration determines how high or low a tone is; the faster the vibration, the higher the **pitch.**

An **octave** is the distance between any given tone and the one produced by a vibration twice that speed. Octaves can be divided into thirteen tones equidistant in pitch; the octave would then be formed by the first and thirteenth tones. The distance from any tone to either of its closest neighbors is called a **half step.** The half step is the smallest recognized difference between two tones.

In our tonal system, differences less than a half step are considered too high or too low in intonation. **Intonation** refers to the degree of adherence to a correct pitch, or playing or singing "in tune."

As the science of mathematics is based on the arrangement of numbers in a decimal system, music is constructed on what we call the scale system. A **scale** is an ascending or descending series of tones arranged in definite order within an octave. The first (and last) tone of a scale is called its keynote or **tonic.** The number of tones in a scale and the distances between them vary according to the particular kind of scale. In a **chromatic** scale the tones are a half step apart. A scale whose tones are two half steps (or one whole step) apart is called a **whole tone** scale:

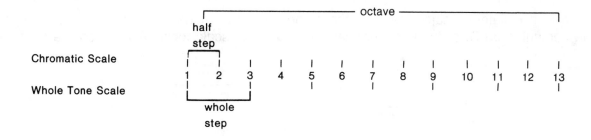

A **diatonic** scale consists of a mixture of half steps and whole steps. The **major** scale, the most common type, consists of eight tones separated by whole steps, with two exceptions: the third and fourth tones and the seventh and eighth tones in a major scale lie only a half step apart. The difference in pitch between two tones is called an **interval.**

| | half step | | half step | |
| Major Scale | 1 2 3 4 5 6 7 8 | | | |

Thus, in a major scale, the interval from 1 to 8 is an octave.

For convenience in singing, we use syllables instead of numbers to denote the tones in a major scale. This system is called **solfeggio.**

1	2	3	4	5	6	7	8
do	re	mi	fa	so	la	ti	do

The black keys on the piano keyboard represent the half steps occurring between those white keys that are a whole step apart, so that if we sound all white and black keys in order, the tones will form a chromatic scale. From one key to the next adjacent key, whether black or white, is a half step. The intervals between B and C and between E and F are half steps, while all the other letter tones are separated by whole steps. Thus, if we start an ascending series of tones on C, the series conforms to the major scale pattern with half steps between 3 and 4 (E and F) and 7 and 8 (B and C).

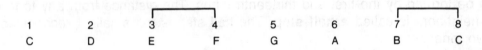

1	2	3	4	5	6	7	8
C	D	E	F	G	A	B	C

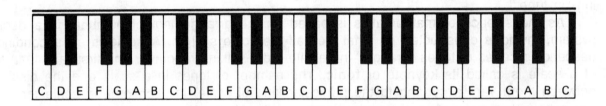

The only diatonic major scale on the piano keyboard made up of all white keys is the scale beginning on C, or the C major scale. The C major scale looks like this on the staff:

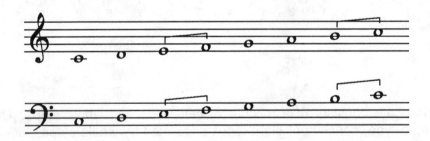

70

Name _____

Date _____

1. What is required to produce a tone? _____

2. What is an octave? _____

_____

3. An octave may be divided into how many tones (including the octave)? _____

4. What is a half step? _____

_____

5. Music is based on what type of system? _____

6. What is a scale? _____

7. What is a chromatic scale? _____

8. What is a whole tone scale? _____

9. How many tones are there in a chromatic scale of one octave (including the octave)?

_____

10. What is meant by intonation? _____

_____

11. What is a diatonic scale? _____

_____

12. How many tones are there in a major scale (including the octave)? _____

13. Where are the half-step intervals in a major scale? _____

14. What syllables correspond to the numbers in a major scale? _____

15. What is the tonic of a scale? _____

16. What is pitch? _____

17. What white keys on the piano keyboard are a half step apart? _____

18. Where is middle C located on the piano keyboard? _____

M A J O R · K E Y · S I G N A T U R E S

Sharps

If we wish to form a major scale using G as the tonic (or the syllable *do*), all the tones will conform to our pattern of half steps and whole steps, with one exception. The seventh step on the scale (F) lies only a half step away from E, the sixth step, and a whole step away from G, the eighth step. To make the pattern conform to that of the major scale, it is necessary to make F sound a half step higher. To indicate this change on the staff, we place a **sharp** sign (♯) directly before the note, and that degree on the staff is then called "F-sharp." On the keyboard, we sound F-sharp by playing the black key between F and G. The major scale we have formed then is called the scale or **key** of G.

For convenience, when using the key of G, we place a ♯ on the top line of the staff just after the clef sign instead of placing one in front of every F on the staff. When such a symbol is placed just after the clef sign, the symbol is called a **key signature.** In the complete signature of any composition, the clef signature comes first, then the key signature, then the time signature. Notice that although the clef and key signatures appear on every staff, the time signature appears only at the beginning of the composition.

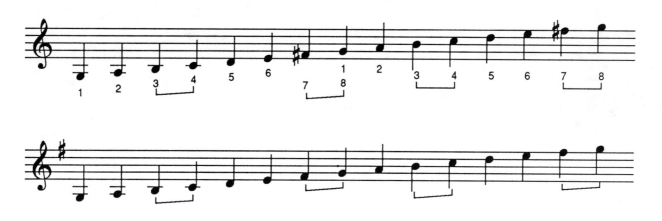

If we now choose D as a keynote or tonic, F and C must both be altered by means of sharps to conform to the major scale pattern. Therefore, the key signature for the scale of D major consists of two sharps. The remaining sharp keys are listed below along with their keynotes.

D major   A major   E major   B major   F♯ major   C♯ major

The sharp keys represented by one to seven sharps are, respectively, G, D, A, E, B, F♯ and C♯. The sharps appear in this order on the staff: F, C, G, D, A, E, and B. It is very important that the sharps in the key signature always be placed in this particular order. The last sharp (the one farthest to the right) will then always be the seventh degree on the scale, or the syllable *ti* from which *do* (the keynote) can readily be ascertained.

To put it another way, the keynote is up one half step from the last sharp. If F-sharp is the only sharp in the key signature, up one half step from F-sharp is G; therefore, it is said to be the key of G. If F-sharp and C-sharp are in the key signature, up one half step from C-sharp is D; therefore, the key is D, and so on.

These key signatures should be thoroughly memorized. The sharps are placed on the bass staff in the same order:

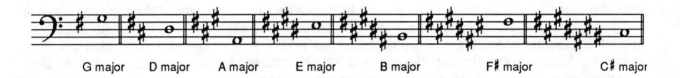

74

WORK · SHEET · 13

Major Scales in Sharp
Keys, Treble Clef

Name _____

Date _____

Write the following scales in treble clef according to the major scale pattern. Indicate half steps with a bracket.

1. Example: Scale of G

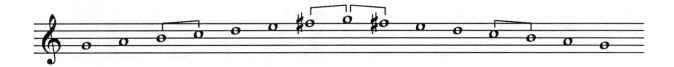

2. Scale of A

3. Scale of F#

4. Scale of B

5. Scale of D

6. Scale of C♯

7. Scale of E

8. Write the key signatures for each of the scales on the previous page.

a. Key of G   b. Key of D   c. Key of A   d. Key of E

e. Key of B   f. Key of F♯   g. Key of C♯

These key signatures must be thoroughly memorized. (Did you use clef signs?)
Staves for practice writing:

Major Scales in Sharp Keys, Bass Clef

Name _____

Date _____

Write the following scales in bass clef according to the major scale pattern. Indicate half steps with a bracket.

1. Example: Scale of G

2. Scale of B

3. Scale of C♯

4. Scale of A

5. Scale of D

6. Scale of E

7. Scale of F♯

8. Write the key signatures for each of the scales above.

a. Key of G   b. Key of D   c. Key of A   d. Key of E

e. Key of B   f. Key of F♯   g. Key of C♯

Staves for practice writing:

1. The syllable name of the last sharp in a key signature is _____

2. What symbol indicates that a natural note is to be raised a half step? _____

3. In major scales other than C, alterations are necessary to maintain the _____

_____

4. Sharps grouped at the beginning of a staff are called _____

5. The difference in pitch between two tones is called _____

6. The third sharp in a key signature is _____

7. The fifth sharp in a key signature is _____

8. The key signature for the key of D major is _____

9. The key signature for the key of E major is _____

10. The key signature for the key of G major is _____

11. Five sharps form the key signature for what key? _____

12. Six sharps form the key signature for what key? _____

13. Seven sharps form the key signature for what key? _____

14. There are how many different sharp scales? _____

15. Where is the sharp symbol placed when it alters a particular note? _____

16. In what order do the components of the complete signature appear? _____

17. Name the sharps as they occur in order in the scale for the key of B. _____

_____

18. In what order on the staff do the seven sharps in key signatures appear?

_____

Flats

Thus far, we have considered the black keys on the piano "sharps" because of their function as other notes "raised" a half step. If we begin a major scale with F as the tonic, we find that B, the fourth tone in the scale, is a whole step (rather than a half step) away from the third tone, A. Thus, to conform to the major scale pattern, it is necessary to sound B one half step lower. To do so, we use the black key previously regarded as A-sharp. Since the notes of the scale must be "spelled" in alphabetical order, we now call the same black key B-flat. We indicate the tone B-flat by the flat sign (♭) placed just before the note B. **Flats** indicate that certain tones are to be sounded a half step lower than the degree upon which they are written.

The key signature for the scale of F consists of one flat.

By the same principle, the other flat scales can be determined.

B♭ major   E♭ major   A♭ major   D♭ major   G♭ major   C♭ major

Flats are placed in the same order on the bass staff.

F major   B♭ major   E♭ major   A♭ major   D♭ major   G♭ major   C♭ major

The flats in their signature order are: B, E, A, D, G, C, and F. The final flat in a key signature will be the fourth degree on the scale, or the syllable *fa,* from which *do* can be determined by counting up or down.

We have another way to determine a flat key quickly by looking at the signature. The next to the last flat, or second flat from the right, is the keynote. (The key of F has to be memorized because there is only one flat in the signature.)

Staves for practice writing:

WORK · SHEET · 15

Major Scales in Flat Keys, Treble Clef

Name _____

Date _____

Write the flat scales in treble clef according to the major scale pattern. Indicate half steps with a bracket.

1. Example: Scale of F

2. Scale of D♭

3. Scale of A♭

4. Scale of E♭

5. Scale of C♭

6. Scale of B♭

7. Scale of G♭

8. Write the key signatures for each of the scales above.

a. Key of F   b. Key of B♭   c. Key of E♭   d. Key of A♭

e. Key of D♭   f. Key of G♭   g. Key of C♭

These key signatures must be thoroughly memorized.
Staves for practice writing:

Major Scales in Flat Keys, Bass Clef

Name _____

Date _____

Write the flat scales in bass clef according to the major scale pattern. Indicate half steps with a bracket.

1. Example: Scale of F

2. Scale of A♭

3. Scale of B♭

4. Scale of G♭

5. Scale of E♭

6. Scale of C♭

7. Scale of D♭

8. Write the key signatures for each of the scales above.

a. Key of F   b. Key of B♭   c. Key of E♭   d. Key of A♭

e. Key of D♭   f. Key of G♭   g. Key of C♭

Staves for practice writing:

S I N G I N G · I N · T H E · M A J O R · M O D E

1. Sing the scale up and down, using the numbers and syllables for the major scale. (Low voices sing an octave lower.)

1	2	3	4	5	6	7	8	7	6	5	4	3	2	1
do	re	mi	fa	so	la	ti	do	ti	la	so	fa	mi	re	do

2. Sing the scale up and down in all other keys within your voice range.
3. Sing the following exercise as written, then in other keys.

1	2	1	1	2	3	2	1	1	2	3	4	3	2	1
do	re	do	do	re	mi	re	do	do	re	mi	fa	mi	re	do

1	2	3	4	5	4	3	2	1	1	2	3	4	5	6	5	4	3	2	1
do	re	mi	fa	so	fa	mi	re	do	do	re	mi	fa	so	la	so	fa	mi	re	do

1	2	3	4	5	6	7	6	5	4	3	2	1
do	re	mi	fa	so	la	ti	la	so	fa	mi	re	do

1	2	3	4	5	6	7	8	7	6	5	4	3	2	1
do	re	mi	fa	so	la	ti	do	ti	la	so	fa	mi	re	do

4. Sing the following exercise as written, then in other keys. (Notice the time signature.)

5. Sing the following exercise as written, then in other keys.

6. In the following exercise, think the pitches in parentheses silently, slowly, in rhythm, as you sing the others aloud. Repeat in other keys.

1	3	1	2	4	2	3	5	3	4	6	4
do	mi	do	re·	fa	re	mi	so	mi	fa	la	fa

5	7	5	6	8	6	7	2	7	8
so	ti	so	la	do	la	ti	re	ti	do

8	6	8	7	5	7	6	4	6	5	3	5
do	la	do	ti	so	ti	la	fa	la	so	mi	so

4	2	4	3	1	3	2	7	2	1
fa	re	fa	mi	do	mi	re	ti	re	do

7. In the following two melodies, write the numbers and syllables of the scale under the notes, then sing. (Notice that each melody starts and ends on the first step of the scale, 1 or *do.*)

a.

b.

8. Many songs use the steps 1, 3, 5 (*do, mi, so*) of the key in which they are written. Some of these songs include "Sweet Betsy from Pike," "On Top of Old Smoky," "The Ash Grove," "Michael, Row the Boat Ashore," and "Morning Has Broken." (See the Song Supplement section.)

   Practice singing the following exercises as written, then in other keys.

a.   b.   c.

2 steps   2   1½

1 3   1   1 3 5 3   1   1 3 5   8 5 3   1
do mi   do   do mi so mi   do   do mi so   do so mi   do

9. The following example is part of an American folk song called "Love Somebody." The first, third, and fifth steps of the scale are used three times in two lines. Write the numbers and syllables under the notes and sing.

10. In many songs, the melody begins on the fifth step of the scale and then goes to the keynote above (5 to 1, or *so* to *do*). Often this fifth step is an anacrusis (upbeat) before the keynote. See "Amazing Grace," "Shenandoah," "Simple Gifts," "The Ash Grove," "Alleluia," and "He's Gone Away" in the Song Supplement section.

The following melody demonstrates ascending the scale from 5 to 1. Write in the other numbers and sing. (Notice that in this song the fifth step is on the first beat of the measure.)

Staves for additional exercises:

Major Scales and the Keyboard

Name _____

Date _____

Write out the major scales indicated by the key signatures and show the relationship of each note to the keyboard.

Example:

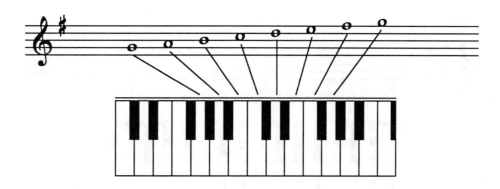

1.

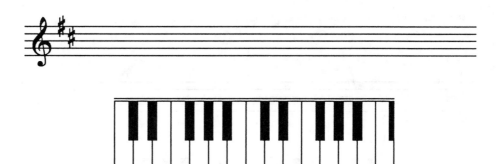

2.

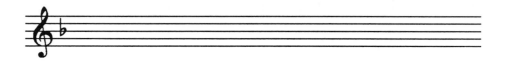

3.

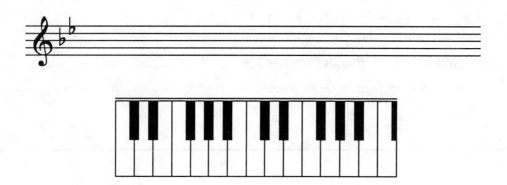

4.

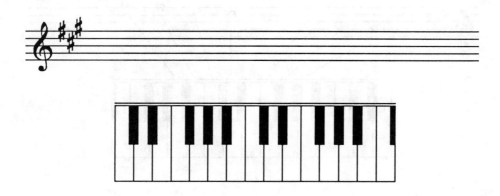

5.

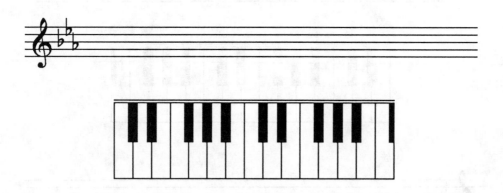

6.

7.

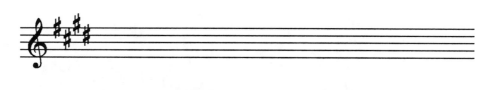

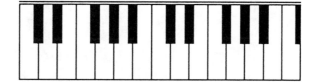

8.

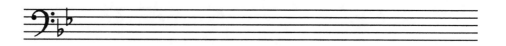

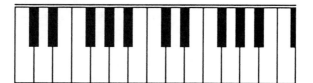

9.

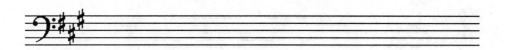

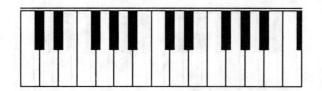

WORK • SHEET • 18

Transposing Melodies

Name _____

Date _____

1. Rewrite (transpose) the melody below to the key of D major.

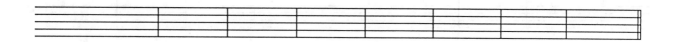

2. Transpose this melody to F major.

3. Transpose this melody to E major.

4. Transpose this melody in bass clef to A major.

5. Transpose this melody in bass clef to B♭ major.

6. Transpose this melody in bass clef to the same key in treble clef.

7. Transpose this bass clef melody to D major in the treble clef.

WORK · SHEET · 19

Melodies in Treble and Bass Clef

Name _____

Date _____

1. Write this melody on the bass staff one octave lower.

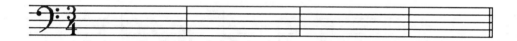

2. Write this melody on the bass staff two octaves lower.

3. Write this melody on the bass staff two octaves lower.

4. Write this melody on the treble staff one octave higher.

5. Write this melody on the treble staff one octave higher.

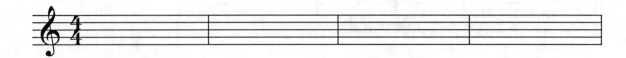

6. Write this melody on the treble staff two octaves higher.

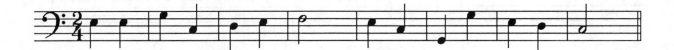

```
┌─────────────────────────────────────────────────────────────┐
│                                                               │
│         ─────────────────────────────────────                │
│                                                               │
│         C  H  R  O  M  A  T  I  C  S                          │
│                                                               │
│         ─────────────────────────────────────                │
│                                                               │
│                                                               │
└─────────────────────────────────────────────────────────────┘
```

Sometimes it is necessary to cancel a sharp or flat for one particular note. To do this, we place a **natural** sign (♮) just before the note on the same degree.

The pitch of an individual note sharped in the key signature can be raised another half step by means of a **double sharp.**

(Same pitch as g')

Similarly, any note already flatted in the key signature can be lowered another half step by means of a **double flat.**

(Same pitch as a')

Like sharps and flats, the double sharp and double flat are canceled by the natural. Sharps, double sharps, flats, double flats, and naturals are called **chromatic signs.** When they are introduced apart from the key signature, they are called **accidentals.**

When sharps, flats, double sharps, double flats, or naturals appear as accidentals, they affect only the notes that immediately follow them on the same degree in the same measure. In other words, the measure bar automatically cancels all accidentals; if the accidental is to be used in the next measure, it must be repeated. Although this rule always holds, a second accidental, canceling the first, may appear after the bar to prevent oversight. For example:

See also page 156.
The syllables used in singing chromatic tones are derived from the syllables for the notes that have been changed. The syllables and their pronunciation are:

Ascending	Descending
do (*doe*)	do (*doe*)
di (*dee*)	ti (*tee*)
re (*ray*)	te (*tay*)
ri (*ree*)	la (*lah*)
mi (*mee*)	le (*lay*)
fa (*fah*)	so (*soh*)
fi (*fee*)	se (*say*)
so (*soh*)	fa (*fah*)
si (*see*)	mi (*mee*)
la (*lah*)	me (*may*)
li (*lee*)	re (*ray*)
ti (*tee*)	ra (*rah*)
do (*doe*)	do (*doe*)

The complete chromatic scale follows:

WORK · SHEET · 20

*Chromatic Scales, Treble
and Bass Clef*

Name _____

Date _____

Fill in the notes and accidentals needed to make the following scales chromatic. The new note should always be on the same line or space as the printed note preceding it.

1.

2.

3.

4.

Staves for practice writing:

WORK · SHEET · 21

*Finding Pitches with Accidentals
on the Keyboard*

Name _____

Date _____

Find each pitch on the scale by drawing a line to the corresponding key on the keyboard.

1.

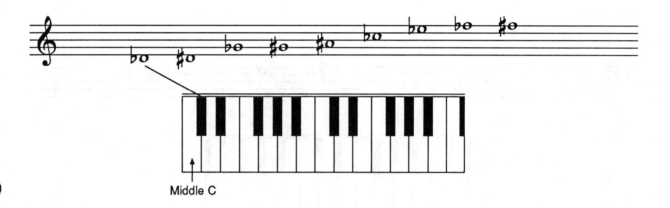

Middle C

2.

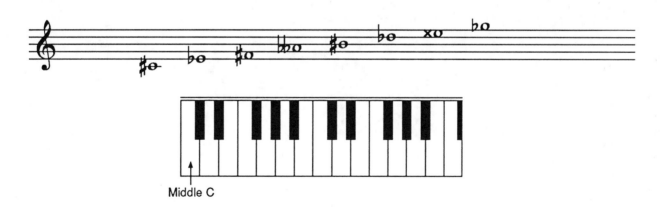

Middle C

3.

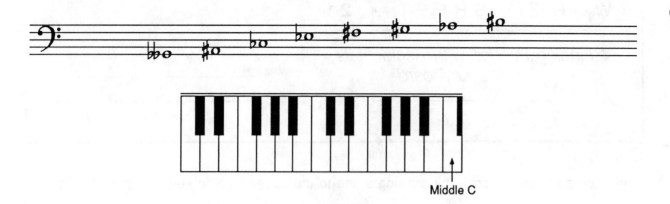

Middle C

4.

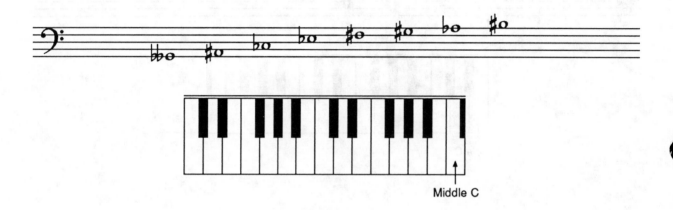

Middle C

1. Sharps, flats, double sharps, double flats, and naturals are called _____

2. The key signature of F is _____

3. The key signature of E♭ is _____

4. The key signature of D♭ is _____

5. The key signature of B♭ is _____

6. The key signature of A♭ is _____

7. The key signature of G♭ is _____

8. The key signature of C♭ is _____

9. Sharps, flats, double sharps, double flats, and naturals introduced apart from the key

   signature are called _____

10. The syllable for the last flat in a key signature is _____

11. A flat or sharp is canceled by a _____

12. To raise a sharped tone one half step, we use a _____

13. To lower a flatted tone one half step, we use a _____

14. There are how many major flat scales? _____

15. What is the order of flats in the key signature? _____

16. How is a flatted tone raised a half step? _____

17. Name the flats as they occur in order in the scale for the key of D♭. _____

18. There are how many major scales in all? _____

19. A flatted tone is raised a whole step by _____

20. A double sharp tone is lowered a half step by _____

```
┌─────────────────────────────────────────────────────────────────┐
│                                                                 │
│   E N H A R M O N I C  •  N O T E S                             │
│                                                                 │
└─────────────────────────────────────────────────────────────────┘
```

Enharmonic Notes

The tone that lies between F and G can be called either F-sharp or G-flat, depending on the scale of which the tone is a part. When two different letter names refer to the same pitch, we say that the two letter names are **enharmonic.** C-flat, then, is the enharmonic note to B; D-sharp is the enharmonic note to E-flat; and so on.

Scales, by the same principle, may also be enharmonic. Thus, the scales of C♯ and D♭ are enharmonic, as are C♭ and B, and F♯ and G♭. Interestingly, the sum of the chromatic signs in the key signatures of two enharmonic scales always equals twelve.

It should be noted that C and F may not be double flatted, and B and E may not be double sharped. Therefore, there are thirty-one possible notes in the chromatic scale:

C	= B♯ or D♭♭		F♯	= G♭
C♯	= D♭		G	= F𝄪 or A♭♭
D	= C𝄪 or E♭♭		G♯	= A♭
D♯	= E♭		A	= G𝄪 or B♭♭
E	= D𝄪 or F♭		A♯	= B♭
F	= E♯ or G♭♭		B	= C♭ or A𝄪

Write the enharmonic notes after each of the following notes.

1.

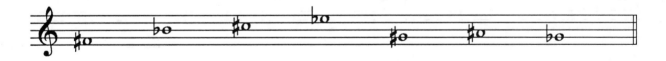

2.

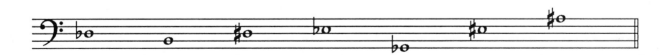

3. The enharmonic notes for each of the following notes may require double sharps or double flats.

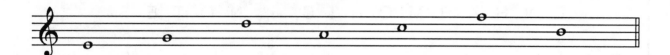

Compare the enharmonic notes on the ascending and descending whole tone scale with the piano keyboard.

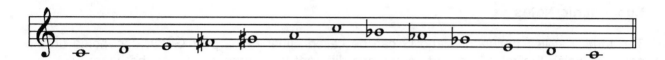

Chromatic signs as used on the keyboard:

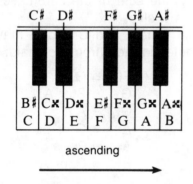

ascending →

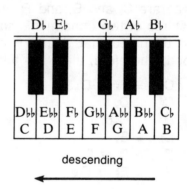

← descending

Staves for practice writing:

CHAPTER 4

T H E · M I N O R · S C A L E

If we begin a new scale on the sixth (instead of the first) tone of any major scale and play the tones in order to the sixth tone in the next higher octave, we form what is called the **relative minor** of the original major scale. Major and minor scales are **relatives** when they have the same key signature. The minor scale is similar to its relative major in many other ways, as well. However, when the scale is renumbered with *la* as 1, the half steps occur in different places, coming between the second and third degrees and the fifth and sixth degrees in the minor scale.

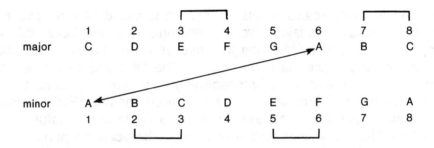

	1	2	3	4	5	6	7	8
major	C	D	E	F	G	A	B	C
minor	A	B	C	D	E	F	G	A
	1	2	3	4	5	6	7	8

This form of the minor scale is called the **natural, pure,** or **unaltered** scale because it comes directly from the major scale. The syllables for the natural minor scale are the same as for the major scale, except that the minor scale begins on *la* instead of *do*.

la	ti	do	re	mi	fa	so	la

The fact that there is a whole step between the seventh and eighth tones makes this particular minor scale sound unfinished. Therefore, we usually play the seventh tone a half step higher (indicated by an accidental). (Later, we see the importance of this, especially in chord progressions.)

						⌜1½ steps⌝	
A	B	C	D	E	F	G#	A
1	2	3	4	5	6	7	8
la	ti	do	re	mi	fa	si	la

This form of the minor scale is called the **harmonic** minor, as it is derived from harmonic usage. The raised seventh tone must always be indicated by an accidental since it has no place in the key signature.

The **melodic** form of the minor scale can be formed from the harmonic. The syllable *so* in the harmonic form is changed to *si* because of the raised seventh. Then, because the interval between *fa* and *si* (equivalent to three half steps) is difficult to sing, the sixth tone *(fa)* is raised a half step during an ascending melody. The raised sixth note is called *fi.* In the descending form of the same scale, the sixth and seventh tones (*fi* and *si*) are lowered one half step to make them conform to the pure minor scale. Thus, although the **melodic** minor ascends with raised sixth and seventh tones, it descends in the natural or pure form of the minor scale.

ascending	1	2	3	4	5	6	7	8
	la	ti	do	re	mi	fi	si	la

descending	8	7	6	5	4	3	2	1
	la	so	fa	mi	re	do	ti	la

This explanation of minor scales is based on what is called "the relative approach." Another approach to the study of scales involves the tonic relationship. In this approach, the harmonic minor scale is formed by lowering the third and sixth tones of the major scale one half step. For example, to produce the C minor scale, the third and sixth tones of the C major scale are lowered (to E-flat and A-flat, respectively). The key signature that most closely matches these alterations (in this case, three flats) is then chosen. (For the harmonic form of the C minor scale, this requires the cancellation of the B-flat in the signature by an accidental wherever necessary.) Thus, any composition in a major key can be performed in the corresponding minor key merely by changing the key signature. The only difference between the two types of scales is that the third and sixth tones are a half step lower in the harmonic minor. The seventh scale step must be a leading tone (a half step from the keynote).

Major and minor scales with the same keynote (such as G major and G minor) have a **parallel** (tonic) relationship; G major is the parallel of G minor, and G minor is the parallel of G major. Naturally, they will have different key signatures, as G minor is the relative minor of B♭ major.

The key signature for a parallel minor has three flats more or three sharps less than the signature for the corresponding major key. In this arithmetical comparison, treat sharps as a positive quantity and flats as a negative quantity. For example, two sharps plus three flats equals one flat; one flat plus three flats equals four flats; or four sharps plus three flats equals one sharp.

In general usage, the word *major* applies to something greater, and the word *minor* applies to something lesser. Thus, it is logical that the major scale has a long third interval, while the minor scale has a short third. (In other words, there are two whole steps between the first and third degrees in the major scale, but just one and one-half steps between the same two degrees in the minor scale.) This difference in the third degree is the main difference between the major and minor scales. We call this a difference in the **modes** of the scales. Music constructed on the major scale is in the major mode, and music based on the minor scale is in the minor mode.

In the preceding examples, the method of solfeggio used was to begin the major scale with *do* and the minor scale with *la.* Another system in use which has merit is to name the first degree of any scale *do* even when changing from major to minor. Notice that the syllables must be changed as the half steps are now in a different position in the scale.

C major   A major

do re mi fa so la ti do   do re mi fa so la ti do

Relative natural minor of C major (parallel natural minor of A major):

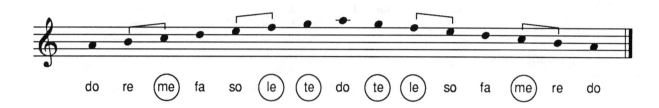

do re (me) fa so (le) (te) do (te) (le) so fa (me) re do

Relative harmonic minor of C major (parallel harmonic minor of A major):

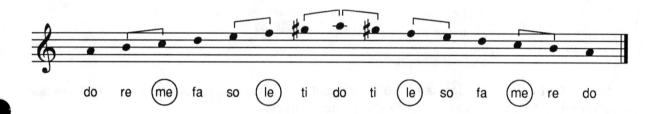

do re (me) fa so (le) ti do ti (le) so fa (me) re do

Relative melodic minor of C major (Parallel melodic minor of A major):

do re (me) fa so la ti do (te) (le) so fa (me) re do

A table comparing the major scale with the three forms of the minor scale follows:

Ascending

major	1	2	3 4		5	6	7 8	
natural minor	1	2 3	4		5 6	7	8	
melodic minor	1	2 3	4		5	6	7 8	
harmonic minor	1	2 3	4		5 6		7 8	

Descending

major	8 7		6	5	4 3		2	1
natural minor	8	7	6 5		4	3 2		1
melodic minor	8	7	6 5		4	3 2		1
harmonic minor	8 7		6 5		4	3 2		1

Notice that in all three forms of the minor scale, the first five ascending notes and the last six descending notes are separated by the same intervals.

S I N G I N G · I N · T H E · M I N O R · M O D E

1. Sing all three forms of the minor as written, then sing in other minor keys. (Low voices sing an octave lower.)

a.

6	7	1	2	3	4	5	6	5	4	3	2	1	7	6
la	ti	do	re	mi	fa	so	la	so	fa	mi	re	do	ti	la
do	re	me	fa	so	le	te	do	te	le	so	fa	me	re	do

b.

6	7	1	2	3	4	5	6	5	4	3	2	1	7	6
la	ti	do	re	mi	fa	si	la	si	fa	mi	re	do	ti	la
do	re	me	fa	so	le	ti	do	ti	le	so	fa	me	re	do

c.

6	7	1	2	3	4	5	6	5	4	3	2	1	7	6
la	ti	do	re	mi	fi	si	la	so	fa	mi	re	do	ti	la
do	re	me	fa	so	la	ti	do	te	le	so	fa	me	re	do

2. Sing the following exercises in C minor, then try them in other minor keys.

   a. Natural minor

   la ti la—la ti do ti la—la ti do re do ti la—la ti do re mi re do ti la—la ti do re mi fa mi re do ti la—la ti do re mi fa so fa mi re do ti la—la ti do re mi fa so la so fa mi re do ti la

   b. Harmonic minor

   la ti la—la ti do ti la—la ti do re do ti la—la ti do re mi re do ti la—la ti do re mi fa mi re do ti la—la ti do re mi fa si fa mi re do ti la—la ti do re mi fa si la si fa mi re do ti la

   c. Melodic minor

   la ti la—la ti do ti la—la ti do re do ti la—la ti do re mi re do ti la—la ti do re mi fa mi re do ti la—la ti do re mi fa so fa mi re do ti la—la ti do re mi fi si la so fa mi re do ti la

3. Sing the following exercises as written, then in other keys.

4. Practice the following ascending and descending scale in D natural minor. (The half steps are indicated.)

Before singing the following melody in D natural minor, mark the half steps and write in the numbers and syllables.

To find songs in minor keys, refer to the Song Supplement section ("Greensleeves," "Black Is the Color," and "Sometimes I Feel like a Motherless Child").

116

Q U E S T I O N S · 7

Name _____

Date _____

1. The tonic or parallel minor of G major is _____

2. The major key that contains four sharps is _____

3. The third note of the C minor scale is _____

4. The relative major of F minor is _____

5. The name of the major scale with no accidentals is _____

6. There are how many major sharp scales? _____

7. The minor scale that contains one flat is _____

8. The pitch of the staff is indicated by _____

9. The third sharp in a key signature is _____

10. The fourth flat in a key signature is _____

11. Two flats form the key signature for what two scales? _____

12. Minor scales begin on what syllable? _____

13. Major and minor scales having the same key signature are _____

14. The major scale that contains five flats is _____

15. The minor scale that contains two sharps is _____

16. Any scale that consists of both whole steps and half steps is called _____

17. Name the major scale whose seventh tone is G. _____

18. Name the major scale whose fourth tone is F♯ . _____

19. Name the minor scale whose third tone is D. _____

20. Name the harmonic minor scale whose seventh tone is B. _____

21. The key signature for the key of F major is _____

22. The key signature for the key of G major is _____

23. The key signature for the key of E♭ minor is _____

24. The key signature for the key of A minor is _____

25. The key signature for the key of C♭ major is _____

WORK · SHEET · 22

Harmonic Minor Scales I

Name _____

Date _____

Examples: C major scale

Harmonic form of A minor scale (relative to C major)

Write the following scales according to the pattern above. (All minor scales should be in the harmonic form.) Write in the key signatures.

1. a. G major scale

    b. Relative minor (harmonic form)

2. a. D major

b. Relative minor

3. a. A major

    b. Relative minor

4. a. E major

    b. Relative minor

5. a. B major

    b. Relative minor

6. a. F♯ major

b. Relative minor

7. a. C♯ major

b. Relative minor

8. a. F major

b. Relative minor

9. a. B♭ major

b. Relative minor

Staves for practice writing:

WORK · SHEET · 23

Harmonic Minor Scales II

Name _____

Date _____

Write the following major scales and the harmonic forms of the relative minors. Write in the key signatures.

1. a. E♭ major

b. Relative minor

2. a. A♭ major

b. Relative minor

3. a. D♭ major

b. Relative minor

4. a. G♭ major

b. Relative minor

5. a. C♭ major

b. Relative minor

Staves for practice writing:

*Harmonic Minor Scales
and the Keyboard*

Name _____

Date _____

Write out the harmonic minor scales indicated by the key signatures, and show the relationship of each note to the keyboard.

1.

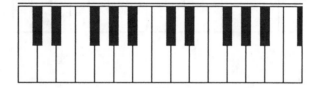

2.

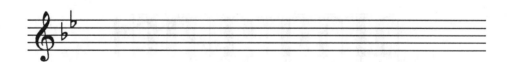

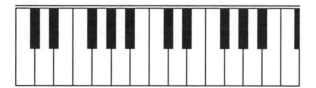

3.

4.

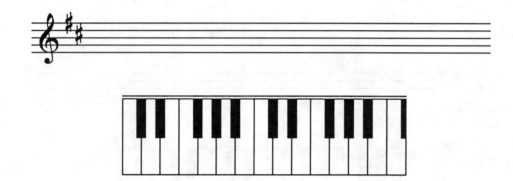

5.

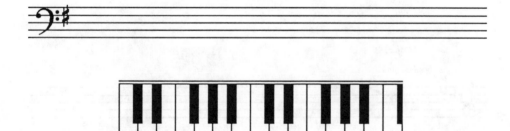

6.

Melodic Minor Scales

Name _____

Date _____

Write the following minor scales in the melodic form according to the pattern.
   Example: E minor (melodic form)

1. A minor

2. B minor

3. F♯ minor

4. D minor

5. C♯ minor

6. F minor

7. G minor

8. C minor

9. D♯ minor

10. B♭ minor

WORK · SHEET · 26

Identification of Major and Minor Key Signatures

Name _____

Date _____

Assume that the notes on the staffs below are the first notes of their respective scales. Write the correct key signatures in front of each note.

1. Major

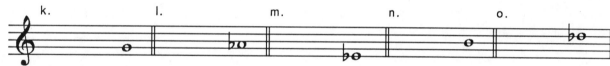

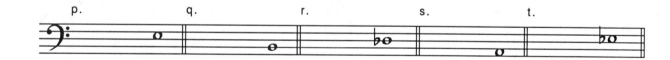

2. Minor

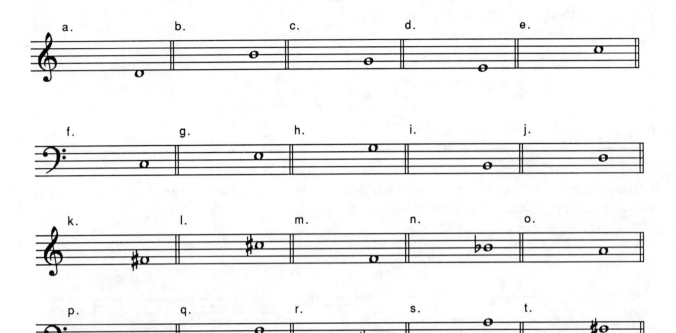

WORK · SHEET · 27

Identification of Major and Minor Keynotes

Name _____

Date _____

Write the correct keynote after each key signature.

1. Major

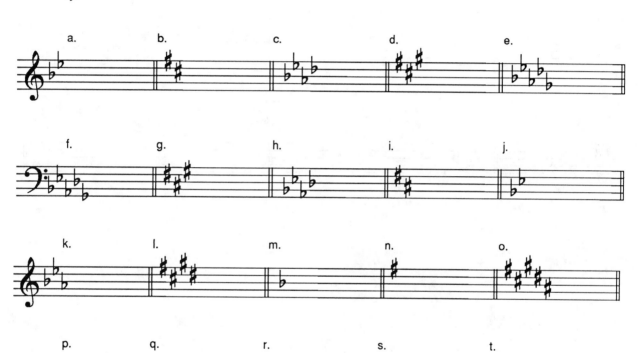

2. Minor

Q U E S T I O N S · 8

Name _____

Date _____

Review of Definitions

Define the following:

1. Tone _____

2. Octave _____

3. Pitch _____

4. Half step _____

5. Scale _____

6. Chromatic _____

7. Whole Step _____

8. Diatonic scale _____

9. Major scale _____

10. Interval _____

11. Tonic _____

12. Time signature _____

13. Staff _____

14. Degrees _____

15. Notes _____

16. Great staff _____

17. Middle C _____

18. Clef _____

19. Bass staff _____

20. Treble staff _____

21. Ledger lines _____

22. Notation _____

23. Natural _____

24. Sharp _____

25. Key signature _____

26. Flat _____

27. Chromatic signs _____

28. Accidentals _____

29. Relative minor _____

30. Normal minor _____

31. Harmonic minor _____

32. Melodic minor _____

33. Mode _____

34. Enharmonic _____

35. Double sharp _____

36. Double flat _____

37. Intonation _____

38. Tie _____

39. Beat _____

40. Triplet _____

41. Rest _____

42. Measure _____

43. Bar _____

44. Syncopated rhythm _____

45. Meter _____

46. Da capo _____

47. Dal segno _____

48. Dots after notes _____

49. Regular rhythm _____

50. Fermata _____

Although most music we hear and study today is written in a major or minor scale, the **pentatonic** (five tone) **scale** is much older. Many examples of this scale can be found in the music of China and Scotland and in American folk songs and spirituals. The pentatonic scale provides the basis for a music-teaching system developed by Carl Orff of Germany and Zoltán Kodály of Hungary, who believed that children learn music more readily through the pentatonic folk songs of their own cultures. This system of instruction is widely used in public schools in many countries.

The black keys of the piano form a pentatonic scale notated with either sharps or flats.

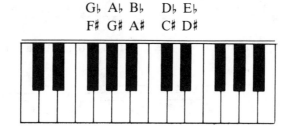

The pentatonic scale is derived by omitting the fourth and seventh degrees of a major scale and can be produced starting on any step of the scale. Therefore, any white key on the piano keyboard can also be the first step.

The keys used beginning on C:

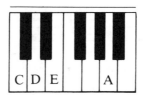

1. Write the pentatonic scale, starting on middle C.

2. Write the pentatonic scale, starting on g'.

3. Write the pentatonic scale, starting on f'.

"Auld Lang Syne" is an example of a folk song written in the pentatonic scale.

"Auld Lang Syne"

Robert Burns
With nostalgia

Scotland

1. Should auld   ac-quaint-ance   be   for-got,   And   nev-er brought to

mind?   Should auld   ac-quaint-ance   be   for-got,   And   days   of auld lang   syne?

Chorus

For   auld___ lang___ syne, my dear, For   auld___ lang___   syne;   We'll

take   a   cup   of   kind-ness yet   for   auld___   lang___   syne.

Other pentatonic songs include "Bury Me Not on the Lone Prairie," "Swing Low, Sweet Chariot," "Goodbye, Old Paint," "Amazing Grace," "Little David Play on Your Harp," "Loch Lomond," "Skye Boat Song," "I've Got Peace Like a River," "Old Dan Tucker," "Do Lord," "I'm Going to Leave Old Texas Now," and "Lonesome Valley."

Because the pentatonic scale has no half steps, there are no strong dissonances. In other words, any two or three notes of the scale played together produce a pleasant sound. For this reason, the pentatonic scale is a good basis for group improvisation.

THE · CIRCLE · OF · KEYS

This chart shows all of the major and minor keys and is known as the circle of fifths or the **circle of keys**. Major keys are usually written in capitals and minors in small letters. Traveling clockwise around the circle, each key contains one more sharp or one less flat than the preceding key. At the bottom of the chart, the enharmonic keys are allowed to overlap since they sound the same. (See page 109 for an explanation of *enharmonic*.)

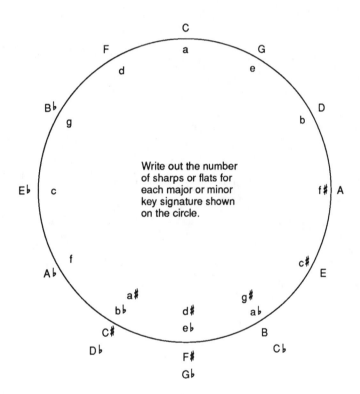

Write out the number of sharps or flats for each major or minor key signature shown on the circle.

An understanding of the circle of keys is necessary in the study of music. The following are several important points to remember:

1. The outer (major) and inner (minor) keys in each pair share the same key signature. These pairs of keys are thus very closely related.
2. Each key differs by only one note from the keys immediately preceding and following it. Adjacent keys are thus closely related.
3. Going clockwise, each keynote (tonic) is the fifth tone, or **dominant**, of the preceding key.

4. Going counterclockwise, each keynote is a fifth below, or the **subdominant** (fourth tone), of the preceding key. (*Dominant* and *subdominant* are explained on page 147.)

The close relationship between major and minor pairs on the circle of keys is demonstrated by the great amount of **modulation** between major and minor keys in music. Similarly, the close relationship between adjacent keys on the circle of keys is demonstrated in music by the great amount of modulation between dominant and subdominant keys. (*Modulation* is explained on page 177.)

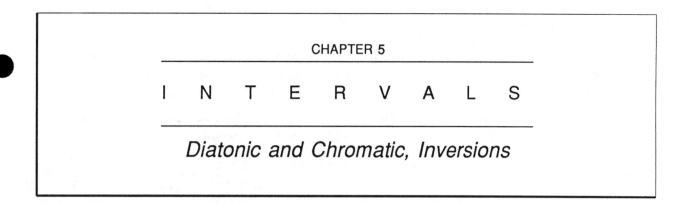

CHAPTER 5

I N T E R V A L S

Diatonic and Chromatic, Inversions

Diatonic Intervals

The pitch relationship between two tones is called an **interval**. When two tones sound on the same pitch, we refer to the interval involved as a **unison**. When two different tones are sounded together at the same time, the interval is **harmonic**. When sounded consecutively, the interval between two different tones is **melodic**.

Intervals are identified in two different ways. The **numerical** name of an interval refers to the comparison of two notes on the staff. Numerically, intervals are counted upward from the scale line of the lower note, with the lower note counted as one. The interval from C to G, then, would be called a fifth, since G is the fifth tone when counting with C as one. An interval of an eighth is always referred to as an **octave**. An interval of an octave or less is a **simple interval**, but an interval of more than an octave is a **compound interval**. (Compound intervals can also be counted upward from the lower note. For example, the second D above middle C is a compound second, but can also be called a ninth.)

The **specific** name of an interval refers to the way the upper tone fits into the scale of the lower tone. When the upper tone falls in the major scale of the lower tone, the interval is said to be **diatonic**. Diatonic intervals are either **major** or **perfect** (labeled with a capital "M" or capital "P" respectively). The major intervals are seconds, thirds, sixths, and sevenths; the perfect intervals are unisons, fourths, fifths, and octaves. *Major* and *perfect* are **specific** names of intervals, while *seconds* and *thirds* are **numerical** names of intervals. Thus, we identify intervals as *major thirds, perfect fifths*, and so on.

In each of the examples below, the upper note lies in the major scale of the lower note. Therefore, these intervals are diatonic.

Notation of Intervals

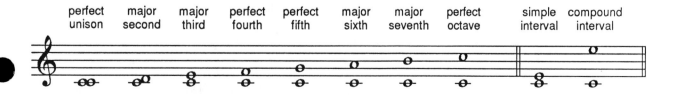

Chromatic Intervals

When the upper or lower tone of an interval is altered by the addition of an accidental, so that it is no longer in the major scale, the interval is **chromatic**. This alteration does not affect the numerical name of the interval, but the specific name of the interval is changed. For example:

1. When a major interval is made a half step smaller by lowering its upper note or raising its lower note, it becomes a **minor** interval (labeled with a small "m").

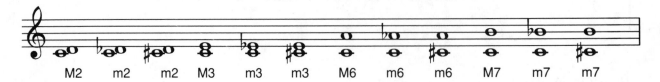

2. When a major interval is made a whole step smaller (or a minor interval is made a half step smaller), it becomes a **diminished** interval (labeled with a small "d").

3. When a perfect interval is made a half step smaller by lowering its upper note or raising its lower note, it becomes a **diminished** interval. (The diminished octave is an uncommon interval.)

4. When either major or perfect intervals are made a half step larger by raising the top note or lowering the bottom note, they become **augmented** intervals (labeled with a capital "A"). (The augmented octave is an uncommon interval.)

144

Enharmonic Intervals

In our system of writing music, it is possible for two intervals to sound alike although written differently. These are called **enharmonic intervals**.

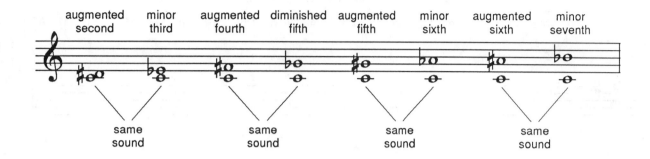

Intervals and Their Inversions

Intervals can use the same tones arranged in different order, with different intervals from the lowest tone. When the lower tone is moved up an octave so that the tone that was higher then becomes the lower tone, the interval is **inverted**.

Both the numerical and specific names of inverted intervals can change. When the basic or lower tone is placed above the higher tones,

1. major intervals become minor;
2. minor intervals become major;
3. perfect intervals remain perfect;
4. augmented intervals become diminished;
5. diminished intervals become augmented.

As each of the following pairs of intervals shows, the sum of any simple interval and its inversion is always nine.

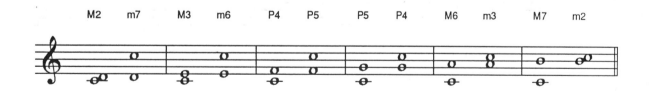

Write the intervals shown in each of the following major keys.

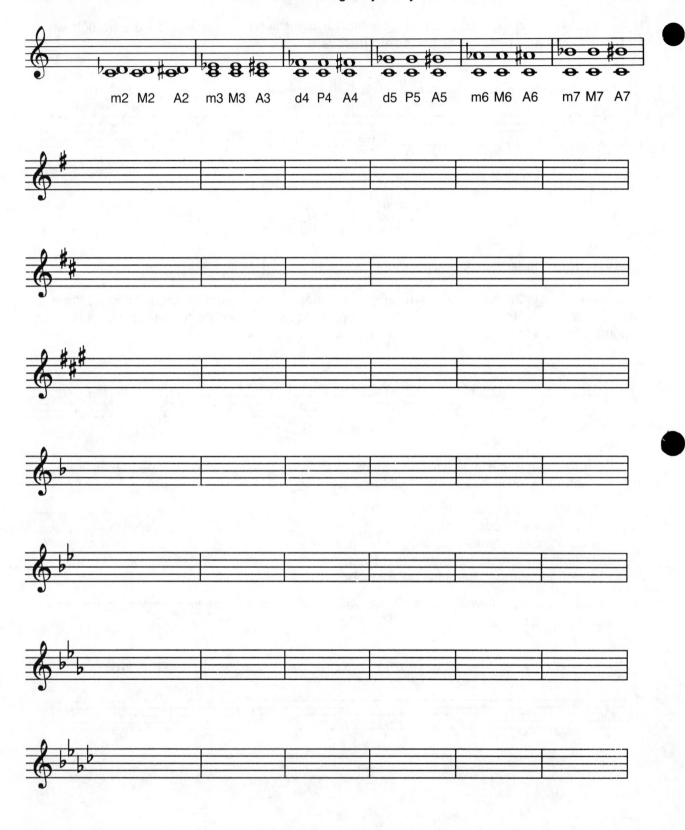

m2 M2 A2 m3 M3 A3 d4 P4 A4 d5 P5 A5 m6 M6 A6 m7 M7 A7

Tone Names

Each tone of a diatonic scale has a name that indicates its position in the scale. The degrees from one to eight are called **tonic, supertonic, mediant, subdominant, dominant, submediant, leading tone,** and **tonic.**

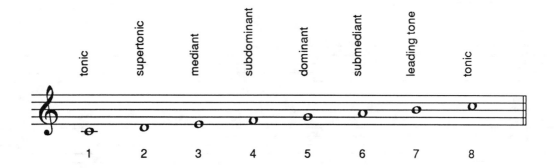

Fill in the chart below with the notes that correspond to the names in the major scales.

Tonic	Dominant	Subdominant	Supertonic	Submediant	Mediant	Leading Tone
C						
G						
D						
A						
E						
B						
F#						
G♭						
D♭						
A♭						
E♭						
B♭						
F						

Staves for practice writing:

Tone Names, Key Signatures,
and Intervals

Name _____

Date _____

1. What is the major key when the

    a. dominant is G? _____

    b. subdominant is B? _____

    c. leading tone is D? _____

    d. mediant is D? _____

    e. submediant is F♯? _____

    f. supertonic is E♭? _____

    g. dominant is F♯? _____

    h. leading tone is B♭? _____

    i. subdominant is C? _____

    j. mediant is A? _____

2. a. Write a simple interval on middle C on the treble staff below.
    b. Write a compound interval on middle C.
    c. Write a perfect unison on G.
    d. Write a major second on C.
    e. Write a major third on A.
    f. Write a major sixth on F.

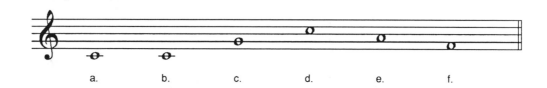

3.   a. Write a major seventh on G on the bass staff below.
      b. Write a perfect fourth on D.
      c. Write a perfect fifth on E♭.
      d. Write a perfect octave on B.
      e. Write a major interval on B♭.
      f. Write a perfect interval on E.

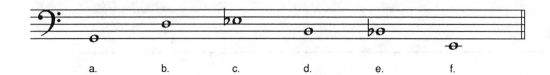

Staves for practice writing:

Melodic Interval Identification

Name _____

Date _____

1. On the staff below, write the key signature for the key of D major. Identify the thirds as major (M) or minor (m).

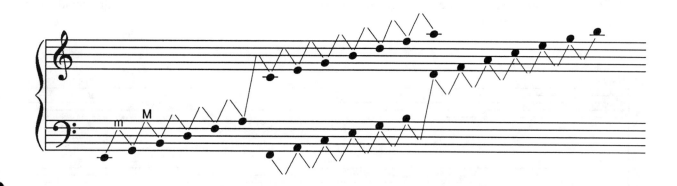

2. On the staff below, write the key signature for the key of E major. Identify the thirds as major (M) or minor (m).

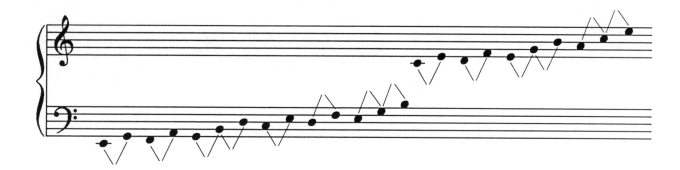

3. On the staff below, write the key signature for the key of B harmonic minor. Add the accidentals and identify the thirds.

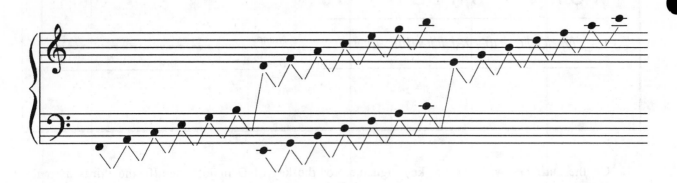

4. On the staff below, write the key signature for the key of G harmonic minor. Add the accidentals and identify the thirds.

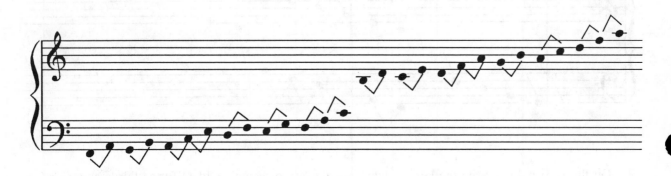

5. Identify the melodic intervals in the following parts of songs.
Example:

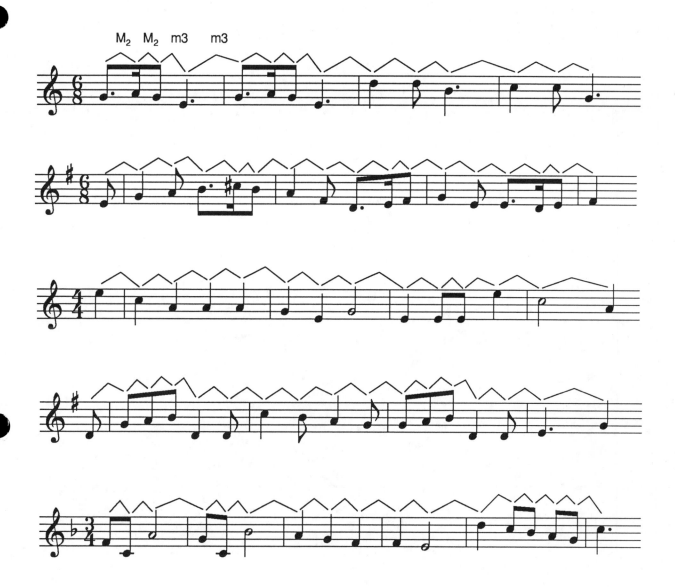

WORK · SHEET · 31

Harmonic Interval Identification

Name _____

Date _____

In the space below the bass staff, identify the intervals. Use a small *c* to indicate compound intervals, as shown (cP4).

1.

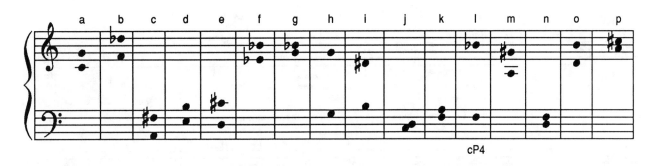

cP4

2.

3.

4.

a b c d e f g h i j k l m n o p

Following is a song for two voices called a *duet*. Complete the harmonic intervals as shown.

Austrian Folk Tune

PU   PU   M3

I count-ed in the heav-en, When the moon shed its light. White

stars that num-bered sev-en, They were twink-ling so bright. I count-ed

one, I count-ed two, I count-ed three, I count-ed four, I count-ed

five, I count-ed six, I count-ed sev-en, Good - night.

WORK • SHEET • 32

Writing Intervals

Name _____

Date _____

1. On the staff below, complete the following intervals:
   a. perfect fifth above B
   b. minor third above D
   c. major sixth above E
   d. minor seventh above F♯
   e. diminished fourth above A♭
   f. augmented second above G
   g. minor sixth above D♯
   h. perfect fourth above G♭
   i. diminished fifth above E♭
   j. diminished seventh above C♯

   a.   b.   c.   d.   e.   f.   g.   h.   i.   j.

2. On the staff below, complete the following intervals:
   a. perfect fifth below E♭
   b. major third below C♯
   c. augmented second below G♯
   d. augmented fourth below B
   e. major seventh below A
   f. minor third below A♭
   g. perfect fourth below D
   h. minor sixth below C
   i. major sixth below D♯
   j. minor second below A♭

   a.   b.   c.   d.   e.   f.   g.   h.   i.   j.

Staves for practice writing:

158

CHAPTER 6

CHORD · CONSTRUCTION

In review, we have learned that sound is vibration; musical sound is regular and continuous vibration; tone is musical sound; and melody, in general, is a succession of musical sounds or tones. When two tones are sounded consecutively, the interval is said to be melodic; when two tones are sounded together, the interval is harmonic. To create harmony, musical tones are sounded simultaneously. **Harmony** is the science of chord construction and progression.

A **chord** is the simultaneous sounding of two or more harmonic intervals. A chord composed of three tones, each a third apart, is called a **triad**. The lowest tone is called the **root**; the middle tone is a third above the root; and the highest tone is a fifth above the root. Any tone of any scale can be considered as the root of a triad, upon which are superimposed its third and fifth.

The triad is named after the position its root takes in the scale. For example, in C major, the tonic triad is C–E–G; the dominant is G–B–D; the subdominant triad is F–A–C; and so on. The triads constructed on the tonic, subdominant, and dominant are called, respectively, I, IV, and V. Roman numerals are used to identify the degree of the scale and to name the chord constructed on that degree. In the major mode, these triads are **major triads**, inasmuch as the interval from the root to the third of each is a major third. The interval from the third to the fifth is a minor third, and the interval from the root to the fifth is a perfect fifth.

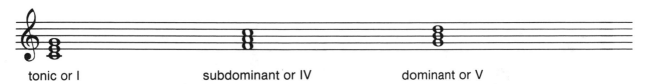

Triads constructed on the supertonic (ii), mediant (iii), and submediant (vi) are **minor triads** because in each the interval from the root to the third is minor. For example, in C major, the ii is D–F–A; the iii is E–G–B; and the vi is A–C–E. The vii or **leading-tone triad** is a diminished triad because the interval from the root to the fifth is diminished (B–D–F). (Notice that the Roman numerals used for these chords are lowercase.)

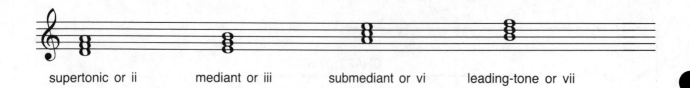

supertonic or ii   mediant or iii   submediant or vi   leading-tone or vii

In the harmonic form of the minor, both V and vii triads are the same as in the major. All the other triads vary.

A triad with the tonic or root tone on the bottom (the lowest position) of the staff is said to be in **root position**. These triad tones can also be **inverted**. Inverting the chord does not change its letter name or the Roman numeral used. A triad with its third on the bottom is in **first inversion**. A triad with its fifth on the bottom is in **second inversion**.

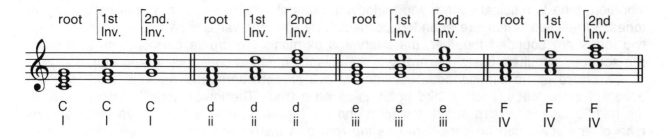

While triads are composed of three tones in superimposed thirds, a **seventh chord** is composed of a triad with another third added. The most common is that built on the dominant (V).

Dominant 7th in:

The process of adjusting effective chords to the basic tones of a melody is called **harmonization**. Many folk songs and familiar songs can be harmonized using only the I, IV, V, and/or V_7 chords. In the following example, the melody of the familiar African song "Kumbaya" was harmonized, using the I, IV, V, and V_7 chords, with inversions of the I, IV, and V_7 chords.

In order to determine the chord to choose in harmonizing a melody, one must examine the key in which the melody is written and then each successive pitch. It is helpful to first write out the three basic chords. The three basic chords for "Kumbaya" follow:

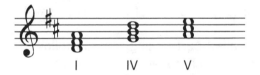

Now look at the melody and identify the pitches.

The first three notes spell the tonic triad, then A is repeated two more times, so we know we can use the tonic triad for the first measure and half of the second. Since B in measure 2 is not in the tonic triad, we need to look for another chord and will see that B is in the middle of the subdominant triad. Therefore, we can use the IV chord on B. In the third measure A returns in the melody, and we will again use the tonic triad.

Measure 4 is exactly like measure 1. Measure 5 is slightly different than measure 2.
insert illustration LA 5.33

---

*There can be a **third inversion** of the dominant seventh chord because there is another note on which to invert.

The pitch G is in the IV chord but F♯ is not. Once again, we look at our three chords and see that we must change back to the I chord. In measure 6, we notice the pitch E that is not in either the I chord or the IV chord but is in the V chord.

Melodically, measures 7, 8, and 9 are exactly like measures 1, 2, and 3.

The second half of measure 10 is a G which is in the IV chord. Measure 11 has F♯ followed by D, both in the I chord, followed by two Es in the V chord, and measure 12 returns to the tonic D.

A V₇ chord was used in measure 11 of the example for variety.

Inversions must be used if the melody pitch is other than the fifth of the chord.

For melodies that use a larger variety of pitches, you will find it helpful to write out the ii, iii, vi, and vii chords.

In choral progressions, called part writing, chords follow one another in logical sequence. In conventional choral style, each chord employs four voices. The melody (usually carried by the highest voice, the soprano) is one part. The other voices, in descending order, are alto, tenor, and bass. If triads are used in the harmonization, it is necessary to use one tone twice in the four-voice arrangement. This is known as **doubling**.

All four-tone chords are dissonant in quality and require, for musical satisfaction, **resolution**; that is, they must progress logically to a chord of consonant character. Such a progression forms a **cadence** and brings the music to a point of repose.

Soprano, alto, tenor, and bass parts are written on the grand staff, with the soprano and tenor parts using stems that go up and alto and bass parts using stems that go down. Which two voices sound the same tone in each chord?

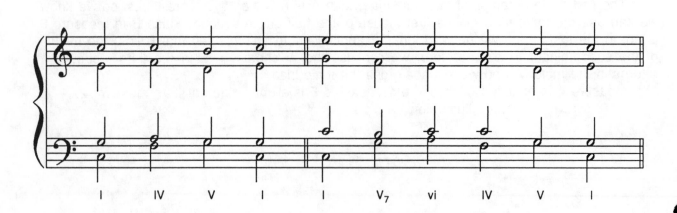

162

Practicing Chord Construction

Think of triads as thirds on thirds. In a major key, the tonic triad is a minor third on a major third. In a minor key, the tonic triad is a major third on a minor third. These are **consonant** triads because they are made up of blending sounds—sounds in agreement. **Dissonant** chords are chords that give a feeling of incompleteness or unrest.

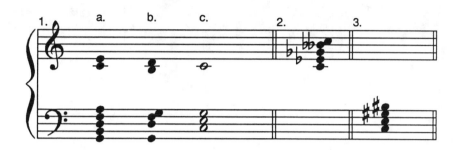

In example 1, play the first chord(a), sounding each individual tone by starting from great G and holding all the notes through e'. You have just played through the **tertian** (or every alternate tone) alphabet. Note that as tones were added, the chord became more dissonant. The full chord contains every tone in the key of C. By progressing to a four-tone chord (b), where the notes G and D are doubled, the sound becomes less dissonant and resolves smoothly to the tonic triad (chord c).

In example 2, minor thirds appear over minor thirds, and only four different notes are used in the chord. In fact, there are only three such chords in our tonal system.

In example 3, major thirds appear over major thirds, and only three different tones are used in the chord since the fourth tone sounds an octave from the first.

The **tertian alphabet**, or **chord alphabet**, should be practiced, beginning on every note, until this alphabet becomes as automatic as the one you use for language. The tertian alphabet is basic to the study of harmony.

Here is a melody for you to harmonize.

Hang down your head Tom Doo – ley,　　Hang down your head and　cry,

Hang down your head Tom Doo – ley,　　Poor boy, you're bound to　die.

Complete the following harmonizing and accompanying chords, then practice, hands separately, on the keyboard. It will be helpful to complete Work sheet 33 first.

Example

I	IV	I	V₇	I
Root	2nd Inv.	Root	1st Inv.	Root

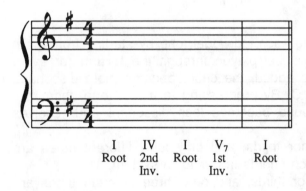

I	IV	I	V₇	I
Root	2nd Inv.	Root	1st Inv.	Root

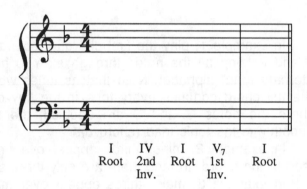

I	IV	I	V₇	I
Root	2nd Inv.	Root	1st Inv.	Root

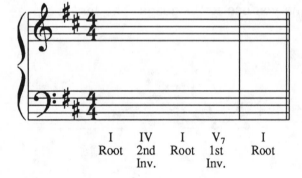

I	IV	I	V₇	I
Root	2nd Inv.	Root	1st Inv.	Root

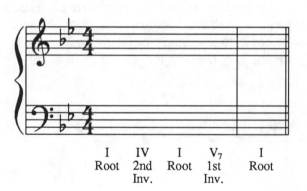

I	IV	I	V₇	I
Root	2nd Inv.	Root	1st Inv.	Root

WORK • SHEET • 33

Chords and Inversions
in Major Keys

Name _____

Date _____

Write the chords indicated. Keep within the staff as much as possible to avoid the addition of too many ledger lines.

Example:

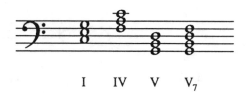

I   IV   V   V₇

1.

I   IV   V   V₇

2.

I   IV   V   V₇

3.

I   IV   V   V₇

4.

I   IV   V   V₇

5.

I   IV   V   V₇

6.

I   IV   V   V₇

7.

I   IV   V   V₇

8.

I   IV   V   V₇

Write the inversions of the tonic chord for each key indicated.

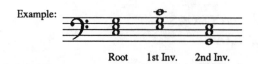

Example:

Root   1st Inv.   2nd Inv.

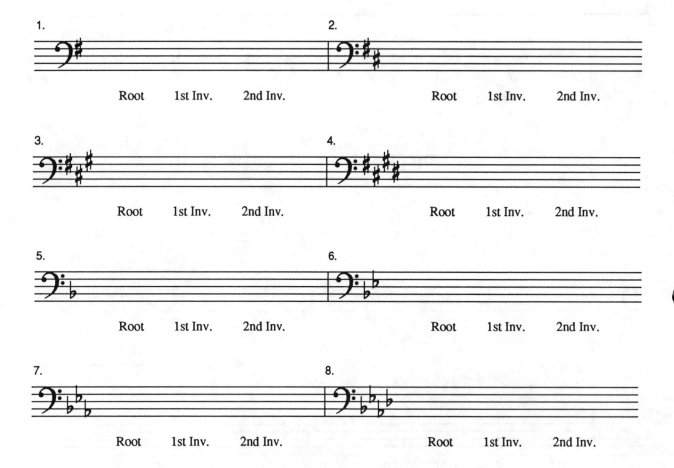

1.

Root   1st Inv.   2nd Inv.

2.

Root   1st Inv.   2nd Inv.

3.

Root   1st Inv.   2nd Inv.

4.

Root   1st Inv.   2nd Inv.

5.

Root   1st Inv.   2nd Inv.

6.

Root   1st Inv.   2nd Inv.

7.

Root   1st Inv.   2nd Inv.

8.

Root   1st Inv.   2nd Inv.

Write the inversion of the tonic chord for each key indicated.

9.

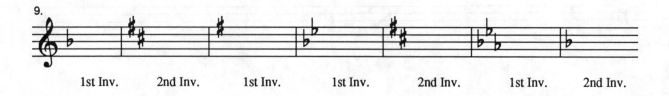

1st Inv.   2nd Inv.   1st Inv.   1st Inv.   2nd Inv.   1st Inv.   2nd Inv.

QUESTIONS · 9

Name _____

Date _____

1. What is a chord? _____

2. What is harmony? _____

3. What is a triad? _____

4. How is a triad constructed? _____

5. How are triads named? _____

6. What are the major triads in a major scale? _____

7. What are the minor triads in a major scale? _____

8. What type of triad is the vii? _____

9. What type of triads are the I and IV in minor keys? _____

10. What type of triads are the ii and vi in minor keys? _____

11. How many voices are employed in conventional choral music? _____

12. What is harmonization? _____

13. What is a seventh chord? _____

14. What are the tones of the dominant seventh chord in G major? _____

    F major? _____ D major? _____

15. What is a cadence? _____

WORK · SHEET · 34

Additional Chords in Major Keys

Name _____

Date _____

Write the chords indicated in the following major keys.

1. Example:

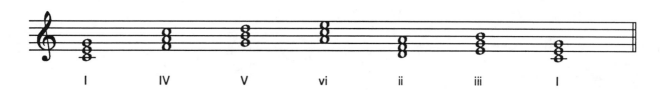

    I   IV   V   vi   ii   iii   I

2.

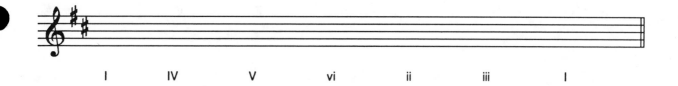

    I   IV   V   vi   ii   iii   I

3.

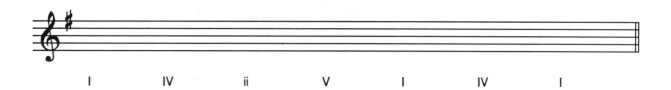

    I   IV   ii   V   I   IV   I

4.

    I   vi   IV   ii   V   I

5.

I   vi   ii   V   IV   I

6.

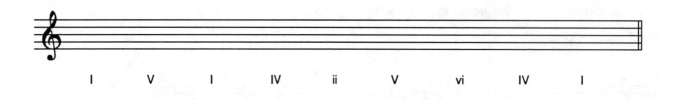

I   V   I   IV   ii   V   vi   IV   I

7.

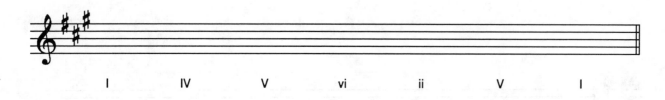

I   IV   V   vi   ii   V   I

8.

I   IV   V   ii   vi   iii   I

9.

I   IV   V   ii   vi   I   V   I

WORK · SHEET · 35

*Harmonizing Major Melodies
in the Bass Clef*

Name _____

Date _____

1. On the bass staff given, write in the chord asked for. Use only one triad of whole notes for each measure. Write them in root position.

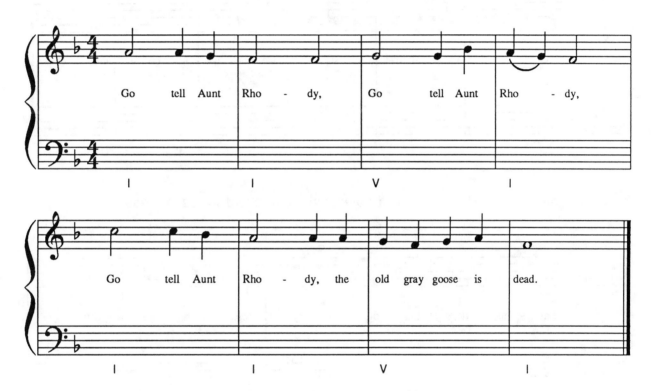

2. On this bass staff, using dotted half notes, write one chord for each measure. (One chord will have *four* notes.)

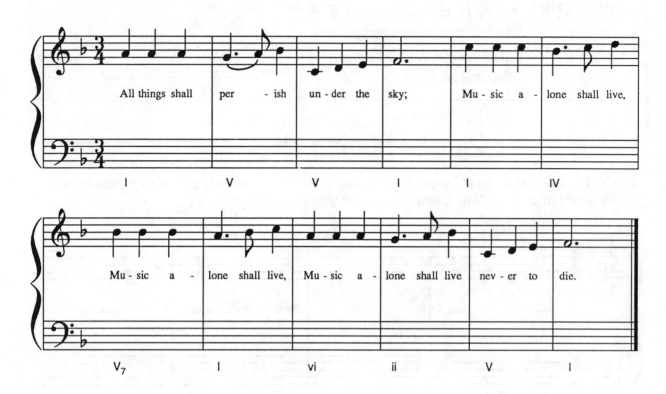

All things shall per - ish un - der the sky; Mu - sic a - lone shall live,

I V V I I IV

Mu - sic a - lone shall live, Mu - sic a - lone shall live nev - er to die.

V₇ I vi ii V I

3. On the bass staff, using dotted half notes, write one chord for each measure.

Lav - en - der's blue dil - ly dil - ly, Rose - mar - y's green.

I I IV I
2nd Inv.

When I am king dil - ly dil - ly, you shall be queen.

IV I V₇ I
2nd Inv. 1st Inv.

Chords in Minor Keys

Name _____

Date _____

Write the chords indicated in the harmonic forms of the following minor keys.

1. Example:

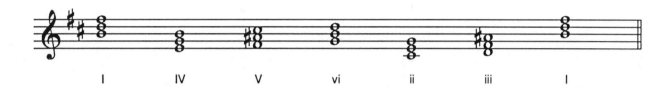

I   IV   V   vi   ii   iii   I

2.

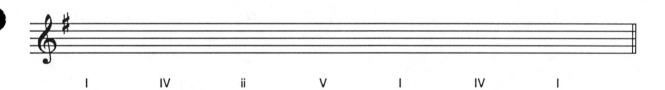

I   IV   ii   V   I   IV   I

3.

I   vi   IV   ii   V   I

4.

I   vi   ii   V   IV   I

5.

I   V   I   IV   ii   V   vi   IV   I

6.

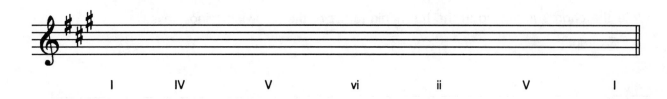

I   IV   V   vi   ii   V   I

7.

I   ii   V   I   vi   IV   ii   V   I

8.

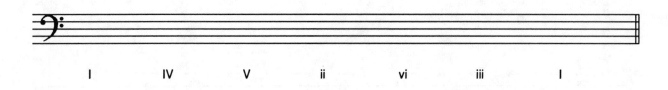

I   IV   V   ii   vi   iii   I

9.

I   IV   V   ii   vi   I   V   I

WORK · SHEET · 37

Harmonizing a Minor Melody in the Bass Clef

Name _____

Date _____

On the bass staff given, write the chord asked for, in the correct rhythm. (This song is in the harmonic minor.)

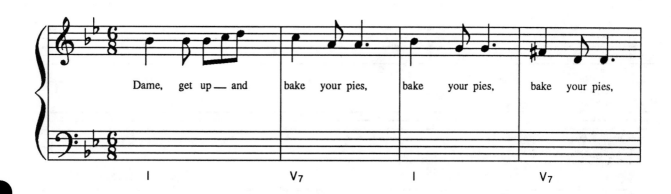

Dame, get up — and | bake your pies, | bake your pies, | bake your pies,

I   V₇   I   V₇

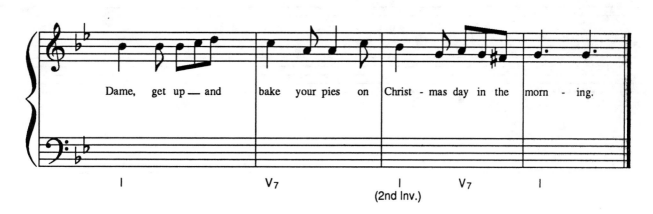

Dame, get up — and | bake your pies on | Christ - mas day in the | morn - ing.

I   V₇   I   V₇   I

(2nd Inv.)

Staves for practice writing:

CHAPTER 7

H A R M O N Y · I

Definition of Terms

By adding another third to the dominant seventh chord, V_7, we obtain a **dominant ninth** chord, V_9, a very useful chord in cadences.

By raising or lowering the tones of a chord with accidentals, we obtain **altered chords** and still remain in the key. Altered chords are a form of chromatic harmony.

A **suspension** is a chord tone that is delayed in its progression to the next chord, thus creating dissonance.

An **anticipation** is a chord tone that advances to the next chord ahead of the chord tones. In other words, an anticipation is the reverse of a suspension.

Passing tones are tones that bridge two chord tones and add interest to the melody.

Modulation is the process of changing keys during a composition.

Transposition is the performance of music in keys other than the key in which the music is written.

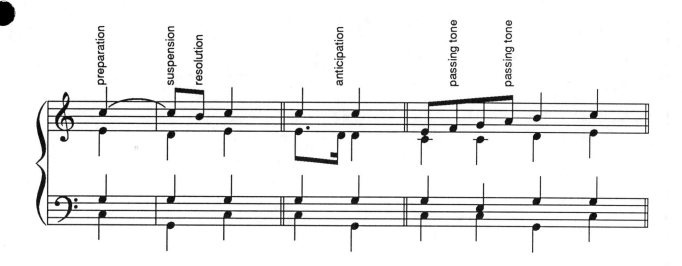

Because this text strives to present the *fundamentals of music* essential to further study, this brief outline of harmony is intended only to provide some terminology in a condensed form. The study of music harmony is an extensive subject requiring advanced texts and involved explanations. It is hoped that serious students of music will continue their study with the help of the many textbooks available and with the guidance of competent teachers.

Characteristics of Chords

The I, IV, and V chords are called the principal chords of the scale. In major keys, they are major chords. The ii, vi, iii, and vii, on the other hand, are regarded as secondary chords. The ii and vi are used more often than the iii and vii. The vii, corresponding to the three top tones of the V_7, is distinctly related to dominant harmony in terms of cadences.

Traditionally, certain progressions of chords have been considered more musically effective than others. For example, the IV chord (often preceded by a I) progresses naturally to the V, as does the ii. Either a IV or ii is frequently used before a vi.

The progression V–I or IV–V–I is called a **perfect cadence** and usually terminates a phrase or composition. The V–vi progression is called a **deceptive cadence**, substituting for V–I. The progression IV–I is a **plagal cadence** and often closes hymns ending with "Amen." The progression IV–V is a **semicadence** and, as its name suggests, it is used to end phrases within a composition.

There are exceptions to these general rules that are used under certain conditions. For example, an additional third can be added to any triad to make it a four-tone or dissonant chord such as the ii_7, IV_7, or V_7. However, these seventh chords sound different because of the varied quality of their intervals. For example, the I_7 and the IV_7 (in major) are more dissonant than the V_7 or ii_7 because the top thirds in the I_7 and the IV_7 are major.

Creating five-toned chords (chords with still another third added), with the exception of the V_9 in root position, adds further dissonant qualities. In four-part harmony, the fifth of a ninth chord is usually omitted; for example, the V_9 in major (GBDFA in the key of C) can be used as GB–FA. This chord sounds the best in root position with G in the bass, or sometimes with the third (B) in the bass, which makes the chord position first inversion.

The descriptions and "rules" above are applicable largely to music of the baroque period (17th century) and, to a lesser extent, in the periods following (the classical and the romantic). Modern music is involved with rules of a different nature, accentuating the elements of dissonance to a high degree. In Bach's day, dissonance was used mostly to contrast with the eventual resolution or with consonant chords. Modern music can be almost totally dissonant.

Modern Harmony

Modern harmony is often constructed on scales different from conventional major and minor scales. For example, the pentatonic scale and the whole tone scale are often used in modern music (refer to pages 137 and 71, respectively). Entirely new systems of composition with new sets of rules have evolved, such as the **tone row** used by Arnold Schoenberg and Alban Berg, among others. Students interested in learning more about contemporary harmonic devices will find an abundance of books dealing with such matters.

Tonality

We have dealt primarily with **tonal** music—music that has a keynote around which an entire piece is built. If the harmony wanders away from this root note, the listener has a feeling of incompleteness until the harmony returns to the key.

The music Americans and Europeans are generally accustomed to hearing has melody and harmony and is usually referred to as "Western" music. However, most of the world's music is melodic and rhythmic only. The classical music of the Orient and the tribal music of Africa and other cultures employs no harmony as we understand this term.

Many countries have been influenced by Western music, as seen in the example of the well known Japanese folk song "Sakura." While it is based on the pentatonic scale, it does have two half steps (C –D and F –G), and although it was originally a melody only, it conveys the feeling of B as the tone center and B minor as the key, lending itself easily to harmonization.

Figured Bass

Since a triad consists of a root, its third, and its fifth (CEG), its intervallic numbers would be $\begin{smallmatrix}5\\3\\1\end{smallmatrix}$, counting upward from the bass. These numbers indicate **root position**. A chord is assumed to be in root position when no other numbers are present.

When the triad is used in its first inversion (EGC), the intervallic numbers would become $\begin{smallmatrix}6\\3\\1\end{smallmatrix}$ (simply abbreviated to $_6$). In the second inversion (GCE), with the fifth of the chord in the bass, the numbers become $\begin{smallmatrix}6\\4\\1\end{smallmatrix}$ (abbreviated to $\begin{smallmatrix}6\\4\end{smallmatrix}$).

In seventh chords, such as the V_7 (GBDF in the key of C), the root position, $\begin{smallmatrix}5\\3\\1\end{smallmatrix}$, is simply abbreviated to $_7$. The first inversion, $\begin{smallmatrix}6\\5\\3\\1\end{smallmatrix}$, is abbreviated to $\begin{smallmatrix}6\\5\end{smallmatrix}$. The second inversion, $\begin{smallmatrix}6\\4\\3\\1\end{smallmatrix}$, is abbreviated to $\begin{smallmatrix}4\\3\end{smallmatrix}$, and the third inversion, with the original seventh in the bass is $\begin{smallmatrix}6\\4\\2\\1\end{smallmatrix}$, abbreviated to $\begin{smallmatrix}4\\2\end{smallmatrix}$ or simply $_2$.

This system of labeling is called **figured bass**. The numerical designations are used only in analysis or study and not in general notation. Keyboard players used figured bass in Bach's day, with the performer improvising with reference to the chords indicated. As an aid to learning harmony, many present-day harmony books also make use of figured bass.

Letter Symbols

In popular music or modern folk music, chord names with no indication of inversions are given as an aid to improvising keyboard or guitar accompaniment. Capital letters indicate a major chord with that letter as the root (C indicates the chord CEG). A capital letter followed by a small "m" indicates a minor triad with the capital letter as the root (Am, then, indicates the chord ACE). A capital letter followed by a "7" indicates a dominant seventh chord with the capital letter as the root (G7 calls for the chord GBDF). "Aura Lee" illustrates the use of letter symbols.

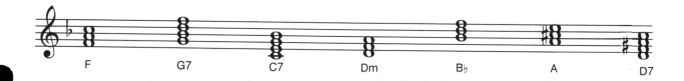

"Aura Lee"

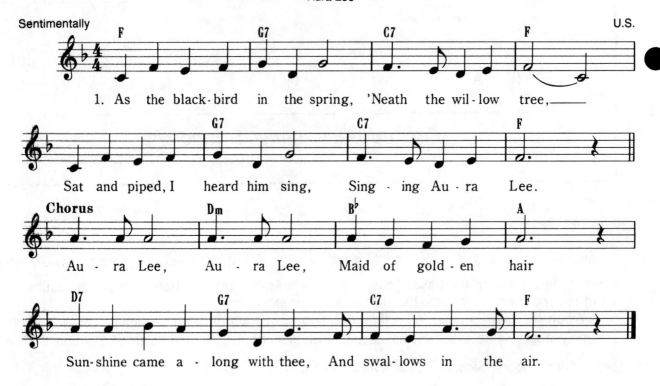

1. As the black-bird in the spring, 'Neath the wil-low tree,_____

Sat and piped, I heard him sing, Sing-ing Au-ra Lee.

Chorus

Au-ra Lee, Au-ra Lee, Maid of gold-en hair

Sun-shine came a-long with thee, And swal-lows in the air.

Source: Leon Dallin and Lynn Dallin, *Heritage Songster*, 2d ed. Copyright © 1980 Wm. C. Brown Publishers, Dubuque, Iowa. All Rights Reserved.

WORK · SHEET · 38

Figured Bass

Name _____

Date _____

Using Roman numerals, label the correct chords for each bass tone.

1.

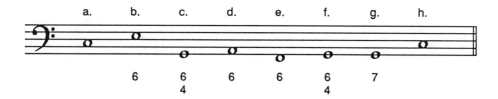

2.

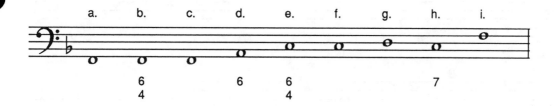

3.

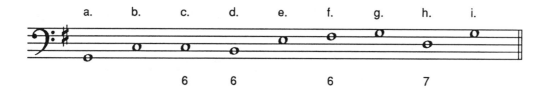

Staves for practice writing:

Melody with Figured Bass

Name _____

Date _____

The melody and bass chords for the Welsh hymn tune "Ar hyd y nos," also known as "All Through the Night," are given for you. Under each bass chord, write the correct Roman numerals and inversion numbers. Because this is intended to be a *visual* exercise, the chords have been kept basically in root position for easier identification.

Staves for writing practice:

Harmonizing from Letter Symbols

Name _____

Date _____

The letter symbols for "Aura Lee" are given. On the bass staff, write in the appropriate chord. Use one whole note chord for each measure, as shown in the first measure.

187

Staves for practice writing:

WORK · SHEET · 41

Harmonizing Songs

Name _____

Date _____

Harmonize the following songs with letter symbols.

"Red River Valley"

Intensely

Cowboy

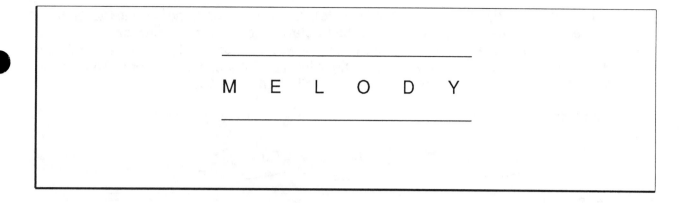

Melody is probably the element of music that is the most personal and the one most easily remembered. One may hear a particularly pleasing melody and go on humming it long after forgetting every pitch, the exact rhythm, or the key in which it was performed. Melody has been defined as a rhythmic series of tones, which is true, but this gives the impression that a haphazard or random succession of pitches results in a melody. In actuality, this series has pattern and logic, with a plan or direction to an end. Melody has pitch, mode, rhythm, **form, contour**, and often an easily recognizable meter, mood, or style, Many melodies sound well when sung or played alone. Others are enhanced by the simultaneous addition of other pitches, melodies, or chords. In this case, the element of harmony would also be important.

A melody can be very simple:

A melody can be complex:

When we hear the melody of "America," we recognize it as being in the major mode, having basically even rhythm, and being in triple meter. The range of pitches used in the entire song is less than an octave, and the intervals from one note to the next is small. Therefore, the contour, or design of the melodic line, is relatively flat.

First phrase A

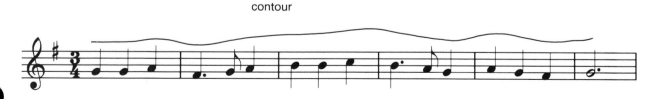

Thus far, the melody starts on G (the keynote), and a cadence brings it back to G in an even number of six measures, with a dotted half note at the end of the **phrase**, or musical thought, contributing to the feeling of a conclusion. However, another slightly longer, and also different yet related, melody continues to a stronger feeling of the end of the song. The form is a simple example of A–B form. Form is discussed further on page 198.

Second phrase B

"The Star Spangled Banner" is also in the major mode and in triple meter. It, however, contains eight phrases and is a little more varied in rhythm than "America." Also, the range of pitches is an octave plus a fifth and there are larger intervals, or skips, in melodic progression. The latter two characteristics make this song difficult for many people to sing.

Pitch range of "America."

Pitch range of "The Star Spangled Banner."

WORK · SHEET · 42

Identifying Phrase, Contour, and Harmony with Given Melody

Name _____

Date _____

In the following song, "The Star Spangled Banner," identify the following:

1. The key—The key is _____
2. The melodic intervals—Continue in the same manner as the example given.
3. The phrases—Over the beginning of each phrase write "phrase 1," "phrase 2," "phrase 3," and so on.
4. The contour—With a pencil or colored pen, connect the note heads.
5. The harmony—On the bass staff given, write the chords that would be used in accompaniment. First, using Roman numerals, write the chords you choose under the bass staff. You may use inversions if you wish. The rhythm must be correct for each measure and may vary depending on the number of chords you choose.

Phrase 1

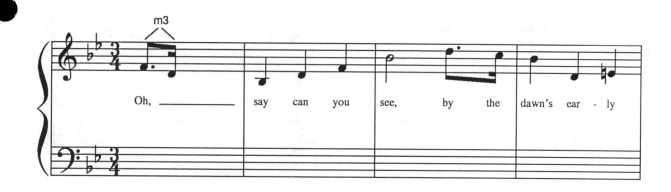

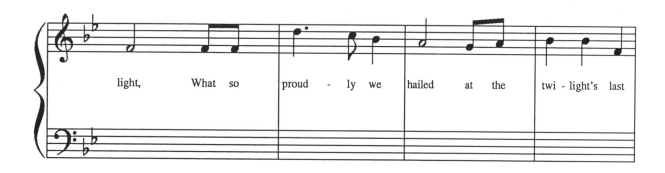

193

gleam - ing, Whose broad stripes and bright stars, through the per - il - ous

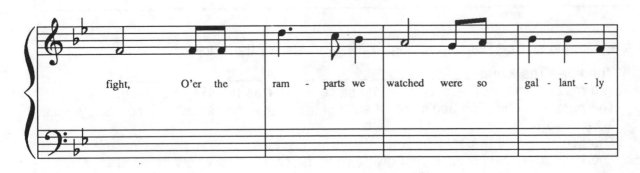

fight, O'er the ram - parts we watched were so gal - lant - ly

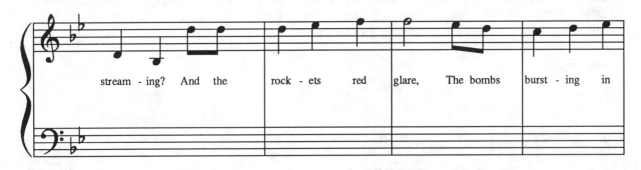

stream - ing? And the rock - ets red glare, The bombs burst - ing in

air, Gave proof through the night that our flag was still

there. Oh, say, does that — Star Span - gled Ban - ner — yet —

wave — O'er the land — of the free and the home of the brave?

Staves for practice writing:

CHAPTER 8

C R E A T I V E · M U S I C

With proper guidance and opportunity for expression, music can be a marvelous source of personal enrichment. Nearly everyone has the desire and even the ability to create music. This is particularly evident in children, whose spontaneous enthusiasm is normally unchecked by comparisons with others or by feelings of inferiority. Recent trends in music education indicate that this enthusiasm deserves careful cultivation.

The understanding of certain rules of structure, balance, and freedom in natural melodic inclinations is valuable in the development of creative skills.

The smallest unit of tones possessing individuality in a melody is a **motive**. For example,

is a simple motive that can be developed into a phrase. A **phrase**, usually two to four measures in length, constitutes half of a **period**, or complete musical sentence. The development of the motive might assume the form of a repetition.

The motive might also take an extended form.

We can call the first phrase in a period the **question phrase**. The second, which often bears close resemblance to the question phrase, we can call the **answer phrase**.

The question and answer phrases should both contain the same number of measures. Melodies usually begin on note 1, 3, or 5 of the scale and usually end on 1 or, less frequently, on 3 or 5.

Complete melodies usually consist of several periods with a definite relationship, often in the form of a direct repetition. The customary form is four periods constructed in a pattern such as A–A–B–A, as in the following example. The first, second, and fourth lines are alike in melody and rhythm. The third line is different.

(This old folk melody, "All Through the Night," comes from Wales and England and can be found in the Song Supplement section.)

The cowboy song "Streets of Laredo" is an example of A–B–A–C form, and the French tune "Ah, Vous Dirai-je Maman" ("Twinkle, Twinkle Little Star") is A–B–A. "Hava Nagila" is A–B–C.

Completing Periods

Name _____

Date _____

Complete the following periods.

1.

2.

3.

4.

5.

6.

7.

8.

9.

10.

Writing Answer Phrases

Name _____

Date _____

Write an answer phrase for each question phrase below.

1.

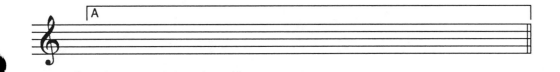

2.

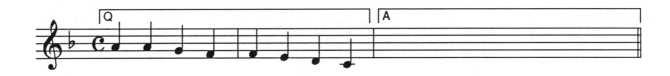

3.

4.

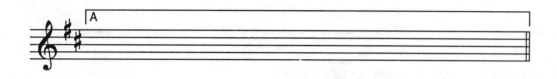

5.

6.

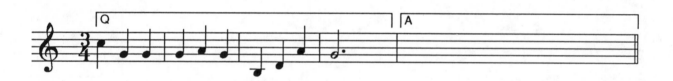

7.

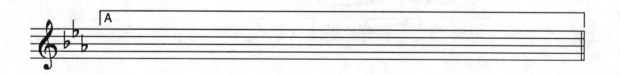

8.

9.

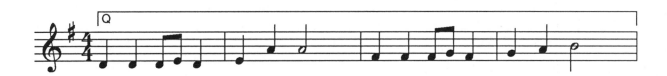

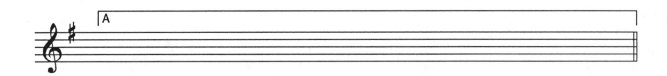

10.

WORK · SHEET · 45

Writing Alternate Answer Phrases

Name _____

Date _____

Write three different answer phrases for each question phrase below. Decide which of your answer phrases you like best.

1.

a.

b.

c.

207

2.

a.

b.

c.

WORK · SHEET · 46

Writing Melodies for Given Rhythms

Name _____

Date _____

Write melodies in the given keys to fit the following rhythms.

1.

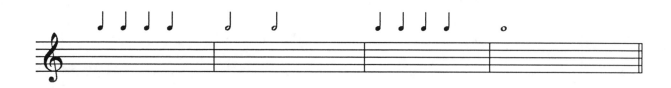

2.

3.

4.

5.

6.

7.

8.

9.

Suggestions for Setting Text to Music

1. Read the words aloud to determine the meter of the poetry.

> Iambic meter—as in mo-tet
>
> Trochaic meter—as in mu-sic
>
> Dactylic meter—as in mel-o-dy

2. Try different music meters with the poetry meter.

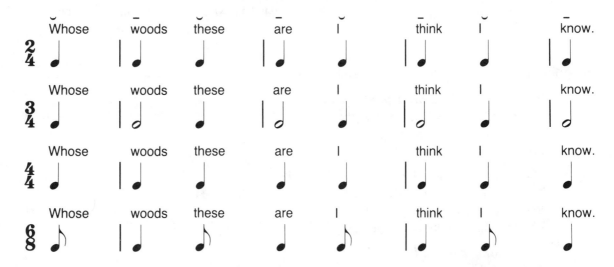

3. Decide on a key. This will be determined by the range of the voice and possible accompanying instrument. Also take into consideration the mood of the words. This will help you decide on a major or minor key. Experiment.
4. Start out with very basic harmony for your melody, using just the I and V or I, IV, and V chords. Start and end the melody with 1, 3, or 5 from the I chord.

In the first example, time was chosen. The key of C and the I, IV, and V chords were used.

In the second example, consideration was given to the mood of the words; the melody was changed slightly; minor chords were added for variety; expression was added; and a slower, calmer pulse meter was used. The key was changed for a higher voice range, making the melody suitable for Autoharp or guitar accompaniment.

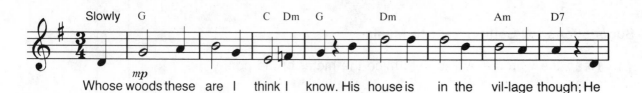

Whose woods these are I think I know. His house is in the vil-lage though; He

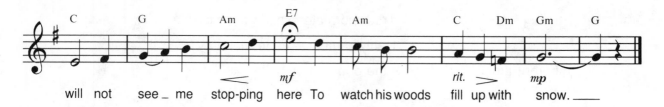

will not see _ me stop-ping here To watch his woods fill up with snow. ___

"Stopping by Woods on a Snowy Evening"

Whose woods these are I think I know.
His house is in the village though;
He will not see me stopping here
To watch his woods fill up with snow.

My little horse must think it queer
To stop without a farmhouse near
Between the woods and frozen lake
The darkest evening of the year.

He gives his harness bells a shake
To ask if there is some mistake.
The only other sound's the sweep
Of easy wind and downy flake.

The woods are lovely, dark and deep.
But I have promises to keep,
And miles to go before I sleep,
And miles to go before I sleep.

From *THE POETRY OF ROBERT FROST* edited by Edward Connery Lathem. Copyright 1923, 1928, © 1969 by Holt, Rinehart and Winston. Copyright 1951, © 1956 by Robert Frost. Reprinted by permission of Henry Holt and Company, Inc.; and by permission of the Estate of Robert Frost and Jonathan Cape Limited, London, England.

The remaining verses go equally well with the same melody, with some change in **tempo** and **dynamics** for variety (see pages 215–217). Meter changes within a line were also tried for effect.

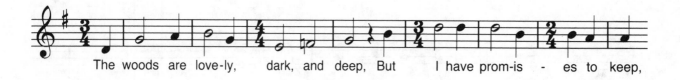

The woods are love-ly, dark, and deep, But I have prom-is - es to keep,

Writing Melodies for Texts

Name _____

Date _____

Select two poem verses from the following list and develop them into songs.

1. *I sing a song of greatness—*
The grandeur in a grain;
Of seas that rim the minim,
Of dust that breeds a plain.

2. *Heaven gives its glimpses only to those*
Not in position to look too close.

3. *Four be the things I am wiser to know:*
Idleness, sorrow, a friend, and a foe.
Four be the things I'd been better without:
Love, curiosity, freckles, and doubt.

4. *Open my ears to music; let*
Me thrill with Spring's first flutes and drums—
But never let me dare forget
The bitter ballads of the slums.

5. *Here in full Light the russet Plains extend*
There wrapt in Clouds the blueish Hills ascend
The groves of Eden, vanish'd now so long,
Live in Description, and look green in Song.

6. *The Pedigree of Honey*
Does not concern the Bee—
A clover, any time, to him,
Is Aristocracy—

T E M P O • D Y N A M I C S • M O O D

Tempo

Tempo is the rate of speed at which a composition is performed.

1. Terms indicating a fixed tempo
   a. Very slow tempo
      largo (*lahr*-go)-stately
      adagio (ah-*dah*-gee-oh)-easily
      lento (*lehn*-toh)-slowly
   b. Moderately slow tempo
      andante (ah-*dahn*—teh)-at a walking pace
      andantino (ahn-dahn-*tee*-no)-slightly faster than *andante*
   c. Moderate tempo
      moderato (moh-dehr-*ah*-toh)
   d. Moderately rapid tempo
      allegretto (ah-leh-*greh*-toh)-a little slower than *allegro*
      allegro (ah-*leh*-groh)-briskly
   e. Very rapid tempo
      con moto (cohn *moh*-toh)-with motion
      vivo (*vee*-voh)-lively
      vivace (vee-*vah*-cheh)-vivacious
      presto (*preh*-stoh)-quick
      presto assai (*preh*-stoh ah-*sah*-ee)-very quick
2. Terms indicating variations in tempo
   a. Terms indicating a more rapid tempo
      (1) Gradual acceleration
      accelerando (ah-cheh-leh-*rahn*-doh)-accelerating
      stringendo (streen-*jen*-doh)-hastening
      poco a poco animato (*poh*-coh ah *poh*-coh ah-nee-*mah*-toh)-little by little with
       growing animation
      (2) Definitely faster tempo at once
      piu allegro (pee-oo ah-*leh*-groh)-more lively
      piu presto (pee-oo *preh*-stoh)-more rapid
      piu mosso (pee-oo *moh*-soh)-more moved, more rapid
      un poco animato (oon *poh*-coh ah-nee-*mah*-toh)-a little animated
   b. Terms indicating a slower tempo
      (1) Gradually slower
      ritardando (ree-tar-*dahn*-doh)-growing slower and slower
      rallentando (rahl-lehn-*tahn*-doh)-gradually slackening in pace
      (2) Definitely slower tempo at once

        piu lento (pee-oo *lehn*-toh)-more slowly

        meno mosso (may-noh *moh*-soh)-less motion

        ritenuto (ree-teh-*noo*-toh)-held back, slower

  (3) Slower tempo combined with an increase in power

        largando (lahr-*gahn*-doh)

        allargando (ahl-lahr-*gahn*-doh)-literally, ''becoming broad''

  (4) Slower tempo combined with a decrease in power

        morendo (moh-*rehn*-doh)-dying away

        calando (cah-*lahn*-doh)-dreceasing in pace and power

3. Miscellaneous terms

        tempo rubato (*tehm*-poh-roo-*bah*-toh)-taken freely

        ad libitum (ahd *lee*-bee-toom)-at pleasure or liberty of performer

        a piacere (ah pee-ah-*cheh*-reh)-at pleasure

        a capriccio (ah cah-*pree*-chee-oh)-whimsical

        agitato (ah-gee-*tah*-toh)-agitated

        tempo giusto (*tehm*-poh gee-*oos*-toh)-in exact tempo

        a tempo (ah *tehm*-poh)-original tempo

        tranquillo (trahn-*kwee*-yo)-tranquilly

        grandioso (grahn-dee-*oh*-zoh)-grandly

        a tempo primo (ah *tehm*-poh *pree*-moh)-at the first tempo

        legato (lay-*gah*-toh)-smoothly connected

        staccato (stah-*cah*-toh)-detached tones

Dynamics and Mood

1. Terms indicating a stable degree of power

        piano (p) (pee-*ah*-noh)-softly

        pianissimo (pp) (pee-ah-*nee*-see-moh)-most softly

        il piu piano (eel pee-oo pee-*ah*-noh)-more softly

        piano assai (pee-*ah*-no ah-*sah*-ee)-very softly

        mezzo piano (mp) (*met*-zoh pee-*ah*-noh)-moderately soft

        forte (f) (*for*-teh)-loudly

        fortissimo (ff) (for-*tee*-see-moh)-most loudly

        mezzo forte (mf) (*meht*-zoh *for*-teh)-moderately loud

2. Terms indicating a change in power

        piu piano (pee-oo pee-*ah*-noh)-more softly

        piu forte (pee-oo *for*-teh)-more loudly

        fortepiano (fp) (for-teh-pee-*ah*-no)-loudly, followed at once by softly

        sforzando (sfz) (sfort-*zahn*-doh)-a single chord or tone accented

        crescendo (cresc.) (cray-*shen*-doh)-becoming louder

        decrescendo (decresc.) (day-cray-*shen*-doh)-becoming softer

        diminuendo (dim.) (dee-meen-yoo-*en*-doh)-becoming softer

        crescendo poco a poco (cray-*shen*-doh *poh*-coh ah *poh*-coh)-becoming louder little by little

        crescendo subito (cray-*shen*-doh *soo*-bee-toh)-becoming louder suddenly

        crescendo molto (cray-*shen*-doh *mohl*-toh)-becoming much louder

        crescendo e diminuendo (cray-*shen*-doh ay dee-meen-yoo-*en*-doh)-gradually louder, then gradually softer

3. Terms indicating a change in both dynamics and tempo

        crescendo ed animando (cray-*shen*-doh ed ah-nee-*mahn*-doh)-becoming louder and faster

        morendo (mohr-*ehn*-doh)-gradually dying away

4. Miscellaneous terms referring to mood

cantabile (cahn-*tah*-bee-leh)-in a singing manner
con amore (cohn ah-*mohr*-eh)-with tenderness
con bravura (cohn brah-*voo*-rah)-with boldness
con energia (cohn ehn-ehr-*gee*-ah)-with energy
con espressione (cohn ehs-pray-see-*oh*-neh)-with expression
espressivo (ehs-pray-*see*-voh)-expressive
con brio (cohn *bree*-oh)-with brilliancy
con fuoco (cohn foo-*oh*-coh)-with fire
con passione (cohn pah-see-*oh*-neh)-with passion
con grazia (cohn *graht*-see-ah)-with grace
con tenerezza (cohn teh-nehr-*eht*-zah)-with tenderness
dolce (*dohl*-cheh)-sweetly and gently
giocoso (gee-oh-*coh*-zoh)-humorously
maestoso (mah-ay-*stoh*-zoh)-majestically
pastorale (pah-stoh-*rahn*-leh)-simple and unaffected
pomposo (pom-*poh*-zoh)-pompously
scherzando (skehrt-*sahn*-doh)-jestingly
sotto voce (*soh*-toh *voh*-cheh)-subdued voice

Song Supplement

"The Ash Grove"

Welsh Tune

1. Down yon-der green val-ley where stream-lets me - an-der, when twi-light_is__ fad-ing I
pen-sive-ly rove, Or at the bright noon-tide in sol-i-tude_ wan-der A-
mid the_ dark_ shades of the lone-ly Ash Grove. 'Twas there while_ the__ black-bird was
joy-ful-ly___ sing-ing, I first met_ my__ dear one, the joy of my heart; A-
round us for glad-ness the blue-bells_ were_ ring-ing. Ah! then lit - tle___
thought I how soon we should part.

2. Still glows the bright sunshine o'er valley and mountain,   With sorrow, deep sorrow, my bosom is laden
   Still warbles the blackbird his note from the tree;   All day I go mourning in search of my love.
   Still trembles the moonbeam on streamlet and fountain,   Ye echoes, O tell me, where is the sweet maiden?
   But what are the beauties of nature to me.   She sleeps 'neath the green turf down by the Ash Grove.

"Shenandoah"

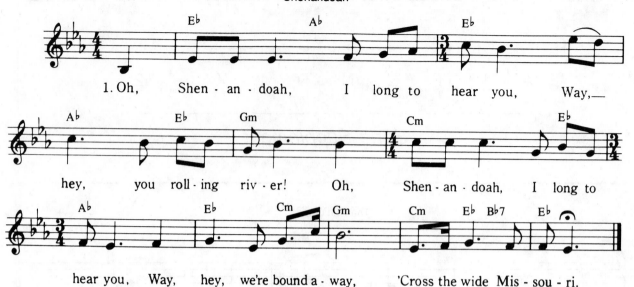

1. Oh, Shen·an·doah, I long to hear you, Way,— hey, you roll·ing riv·er! Oh, Shen·an·doah, I long to hear you, Way, hey, we're bound a·way, 'Cross the wide Mis·sou·ri.

2. O, Shenandoah, I love your daughter,
   Way, hay, you rolling river,
   Oh, Shenandoah, I love your daughter,
   Way, hay, we're bound away,
   'Cross the wide Missouri.

3. Oh, Shenandoah, I love her truly,
   Way, hay, you rolling river,
   Oh, Shenandoah, I love her truly,
   Way, hay, we're bound away,
   'Cross the wide Missouri.

4. I long to see your fertile valley,
   Way, hay, you rolling river,
   I long to see your fertile valley,
   Way, hay, we're bound away,
   'Cross the wide Missouri.

5. Oh, Shenandoah, I'm bound to leave you,
   Way, hay, you rolling river,
   Oh, Shenandoah, I'm bound to leave you,
   Way, hay, we're bound away,
   'Cross the wide Missouri.

Source: Leon Dallin and Lynn Dallin, *Heritage Songster*, 2d ed. Copyright © 1980 Wm. C. Brown Publishers, Dubuque, Iowa. All Rights Reserved.

"Alleluia"

Traditional melody

Al - le - lu - ia, al - le - lu - ia, al - le - lu - ia, al - le - lu - ia, al - le -

lu - ia, al - le - lu - ia, Al - le - lu - ia, al - le - lu - ia!

"Streets of Laredo"

Woefully

Cowboy

1. As I____ walked out in the streets of La - re - do, As

I____ walked out in La - re - do one day, I

spied a young cow - boy all wrapped in white lin - en, All

wrapped in white lin - en as cold as the clay.

2. "I see by your outfit that you are a cowboy,"
   These words he did say as I boldly stepped by;
   "Come, sit down beside me and hear my sad story,
   I'm shot in the breast and I'm going to die."

3. "Now once in the saddle I used to go dashing,
   Yes, once in the saddle I used to be gay,
   I'd dress myself up and go down to the card-house,
   I got myself shot and I'm dying today."

4. "Get six husky cowboys to carry my coffin,
   Get ten lovely maidens to sing me a song,
   And beat the drum slowly and play the fife lowly,
   For I'm a young cowboy who knows he was wrong."

Source: Leon Dallin and Lynn Dallin, *Heritage Songster*, 2d ed. Copyright © 1980 Wm. C. Brown Publishers, Dubuque, Iowa.
All Rights Reserved.

5. *"Oh, please go and bring me a cup of cold water*
   To cool my parched lips, they are burning," he said,
   Before I could get it, his soul had departed
   And gone to its Maker, the cowboy was dead.

6. *We beat the drum slowly and played the fife lowly*
   And wept in our grief as we bore him along,
   For we loved the cowboy, so brave and so handsome,
   We loved that young cowboy although he'd done wrong.

The melody of this song is similar to a popular, old Irish folk air, "Bard of Armagh," which probably was adapted by sentimental cowboys to fit their own experiences and locale.

"Passing By"

1. There is a la - dy sweet and kind,

Was nev - er face so pleased my___ mind;

I did but see her pass - ing by, And

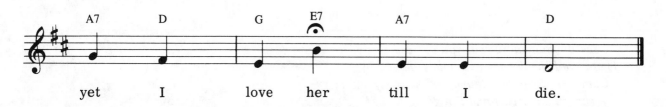

yet I love her till I die.

2. *Her gesture, motion, and her smile,*
   Her wit, her voice, my heart beguiles,
   Beguiles my heart, I know not why,
   And yet I love her till I die.

3. *Cupid is winged and doth range*
   Her country, so my love doth change.
   But change the earth, or change the sky,
   Yet will I love her till I die.

Source: Leon Dallin and Lynn Dallin, *Folk Songster*. Copyright © 1967 Wm. C. Brown Publishers, Dubuque, Iowa. All Rights Reserved.

Eleanor Farjeon

Gaelic melody

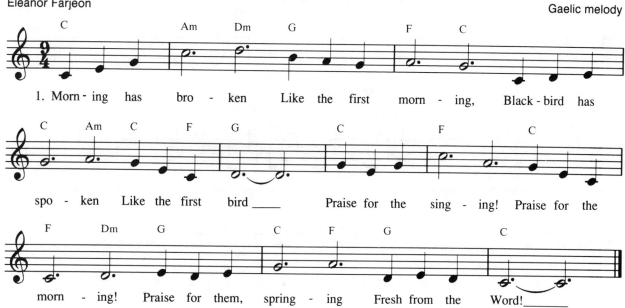

1. Morn - ing has bro - ken Like the first morn - ing, Black - bird has
spo - ken Like the first bird ____ Praise for the sing - ing! Praise for the
morn - ing! Praise for them, spring - ing Fresh from the Word! ____

2. *Sweet the rain's new fall,*
   Sunlit from heaven,
   Like the first dewfall
   On the first grass.
   Praise for the sweetness
   Of the wet garden,
   Sprung in completeness
   Where his feet pass.

3. *Mine is the sunlight!*
   Mine is the morning
   Born of the one light
   Eden saw play!
   Praise with elation,
   Praise every morning,
   God's re-creation
   Of the new day!

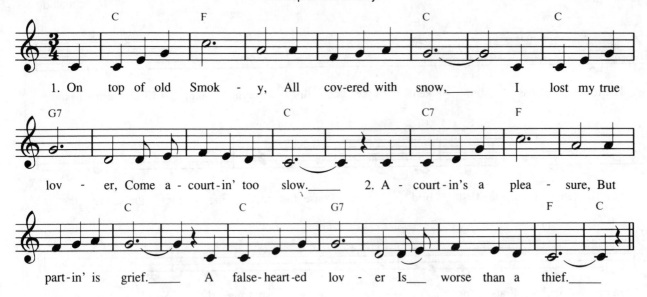

1. On top of old Smok - y, All cov-ered with snow,____ I lost my true lov - er, Come a - court-in' too slow.____ 2. A - court - in's a plea - sure, But part-in' is grief.____ A false-heart-ed lov - er Is__ worse than a thief.____

3. *A thief, he will rob you*
   And take what you have,
   But a false-hearted lover
   Will send you to your grave.

4. *He'll hug you and kiss you*
   And tell you more lies
   Than the cross ties on a railroad
   Or the stars in the skies.

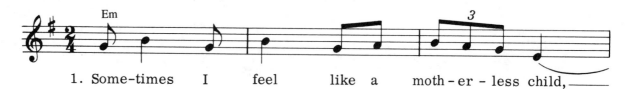

1. Some-times I feel like a moth-er-less child, _____

_____ Some-times I feel like a moth-er-less child, _____

_____ Some-times I feel like a moth-er-less child, _____

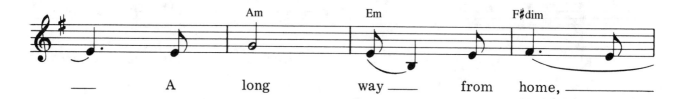

_____ A long way _____ from home, _____

_____ a long way _____ from home. _____

2. Sometimes I feel like I'm almost gone, [three times]
   A long way from home, a long way from home.

3. Sometimes I feel that the night is long, [three times]
   A long way from home, a long way from home.

4. Sometimes I feel that I haven't a friend, [three times]
   A long way from home, a long way from home.

Source: Leon Dallin and Lynn Dallin, *Folk Songster*. Copyright © 1967 Wm. C. Brown Publishers, Dubuque, Iowa. All Rights Reserved.

"He's Gone Away"

1. I'm goin' a - way___ for to stay a lit - tle while, ___
___ But I'm com-ing back ___ if I go ten thou - sand miles. ___
___ Oh, who will tie ___ your shoes? ___ And who will
glove ___ your hand? ___ And who will kiss those ru - by
lips when I am gone? ___ Look a -
way, ___ look a - way o - ver Yan - dro. ___

2. He's gone away for to stay a little while,
But he's coming back if he goes ten thousand miles.
Oh, daddy'll tie my shoes,
And mommy'll glove my hands,
And you will kiss my ruby lips when you come back!
Look away, look away over Yandro.

Source: Leon Dallin and Lynn Dallin, *Folk Songster*. Copyright © 1967 Wm. C. Brown Publishers, Dubuque, Iowa. All Rights Reserved.

"The Sally Gardens"

Words by W. B. Yeats

Irish tune

1. Down___ by the__ Sal - ly___ gar - dens my___ love and___ I did meet, She__

passed the__ Sal - ly___ gar - dens with___ lit - tle__ snow-white feet. She bid me__ take love

eas - y, as the leaves grow___ on___ the__ tree, But___ I be - ing young and___

fool - ish with___ her did___ not a - gree.

2. *In a field by the river my love and I did stand,*
   And on my leaning shoulder she laid her snow-white hand;
   She bid me take life easy as the grass grows on the weirs,
   But I was young and foolish, and now am full of tears.

"Michael, Row the Boat Ashore"

Mi-chael, row the boat a - shore, Hal - le - lu - jah! Mi-chael, row the boat a -

shore, Hal- le - lu - jah.

"Black Is the Color"

1. Black, black, black is the col-or of my true love's hair, Her

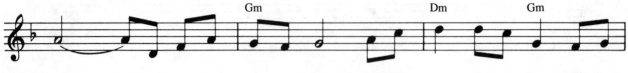

lips ——— are won-drous ros-y fair, And the pret - ti-est face and the

dain - ti-est hands, I love ——— the ground where-on she stands.

2. Oh, I love my love, and well she knows,
   I love the grass whereon she goes,
   If she on earth no more I see,
   My life would fade away from me.

3. I go to Troublesome to mourn and weep,
   But satisfied I ne'er can sleep,
   I'll write her a note in a few little lines,
   I'll suffer death a thousand times.   [repeat verse 1]

"Sweet Betsy from Pike"

"Greensleeves"

Quietly   England

1. A - las my love_ you do me wrong,_ To cast me off _ dis-courte-ous-ly;   And
I have loved_ you for so long,_ De - light - ing in_ your com-pa - ny

Green - sleeves_ was all my joy,____ Green - sleeves_ was my de - light,

Green - sleeves was my heart of gold,_ And who but my la - dy Green - sleeves.

"Love Somebody"

With zest

United States

Love some-bod-y, yes I do, Love some-bod-y, yes I do, Love some-bod-y, yes I do, Love some-bod-y but I won't tell who.

Chorus

Love some-bod-y, yes I do, Love some-bod-y, yes I do, Love some-bod-y, yes I do, And I hope some-bod-y loves me too.

Source: Leon Dallin and Lynn Dallin, *Heritage Songster*, 2d ed. Copyright © 1980 Wm. C. Brown Publishers, Dubuque, Iowa. All Rights Reserved.

"Dona Nobis Pacem"

Peacefully   Round

Do - na   no - bis   pa - cem pa - cem,

do - na __ no - bis   pa - __ - cem.

Do - na   no - bis   pa - cem,

do - na   no - bis   pa - __ - cem.

Do - na   no - bis __ pa - cem,

do - na   no - bis   pa - __ - cem.

Serenely   Wales and England

1. Sleep, my child and peace at-tend thee, All through the night;

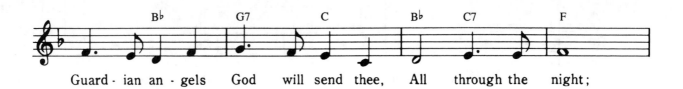

Guard-ian an-gels God will send thee, All through the night;

Soft the drows-y hours are creep-ing, Hill and vale in slum-ber steep-ing;

I my lov-ing vig-il keep-ing, All through the night.

2. While the moon her watch is keeping
    All through the night;
    While the weary world is sleeping
    All through the night;
    O'er thy spirit gently stealing,
    Visions of delight revealing,
    Breathes a pure and holy feeling
    All through the night.

Source: Leon Dallin and Lynn Dallin, *Heritage Songster*, 2d ed. Copyright © 1980 Wm. C. Brown Publishers, Dubuque, Iowa. All Rights Reserved.

"Simple Gifts"

Shaker hymn

'Tis a gift to be sim - ple, 'tis a gift to be free, 'Tis a

gift to come down where we ought to be; And when we find our-selves in the

place just right, 'Twill be in the val - ley of love and de - light.

When true sim - plic - i - ty is gained, To bow and to bend we___ shan't be a - shamed; To

turn, turn will be our de - light, Till by turn - ing, turn - ing we come round right.

Source: From *Hymnal for Contemporary Christians*, Singspiration Music, Zondervan Publishing House.

"The Tailor and the Mouse"

With spirit

England

1. There was a tai-lor had a mouse, Hi did-dle um-kum fee - dle. They

lived to-geth-er in one house, Hi did-dle um-kum fee - dle.

Chorus

Hi did-dle um-kum ta-rum tan-tum, Through the town of Ram - say,

Hi did-dle um-kum, o - ver the lea, Hi did-dle um-kum fee - dle.

2. The tailor thought the mouse was ill,
Hi diddle umkum feedle,
Because he took an awful chill,
Hi diddle umkum feedle.

3. The tailor thought his mouse would die,
Hi diddle umkum feedle,
And so he baked him in a pie,
Hi diddle umkum feedle.

4. He cut the pie, the mouse ran out,
Hi diddle umkum feedle,
The mouse was in a terrible pout,
Hi diddle umkum feedle.

5. The tailor gave him catnip tea,
Hi diddle umkum feedle,
Until a healthy mouse was he,
Hi diddle umkum feedle.

Source: Leon Dallin and Lynn Dallin, *Heritage Songster*, 2d ed. Copyright © 1980 Wm. C. Brown Publishers, Dubuque, Iowa.
All Rights Reserved.

Plaintively   Southern U.S.

1. What won-drous love is this, O my soul, O my
soul! What won-drous love is this, O my soul!_____ What
won-drous love is this that caused the Lord_ of bliss To
send this bless-ed gift for my soul, for my soul, To
send this bless-ed gift for my soul:_____

2. *When I was sinking down, sinking down, sinking down,*
   When I was sinking down, sinking down;
   When I was sinking down beneath God's righteous frown,
   Christ laid aside His crown for my soul, for my soul,
   Christ laid aside His crown for my soul.

3. *And when from death I'm free, I'll sing on, I'll sing on,*
   And when from death I'm free, I'll sing on;
   And when from death I'm free, I'll sing and joyful be,
   And through eternity I'll sing on, I'll sing on,
   And through eternity I'll sing on.

Franz Gruber
Joseph Mohr

Peacefully

1. Si - lent night, ho - ly night! All is calm, all is bright.

Round yon vir - gin Moth - er and Child. Ho - ly In - fant so ten - der and mild,

Sleep in heav - en - ly peace,_____ Sleep__ in heav - en - ly peace.

2. Silent night, holy night!
   Shepherds quake at the sight.
   Glories stream from heaven afar,
   Heavenly hosts sing, "Alleluia!"
   Christ, the Saviour is born,
   Christ, the Saviour is born.

3. Silent night, holy night!
   Son of God, love's pure light!
   Radiant beams from Thy holy face
   With the dawn of redeeming grace,
   Jesus, Lord, at Thy birth,
   Jesus, Lord, at Thy birth.

1. Stille Nacht, Heilige Nacht! Alles schläft, einsam wacht
   Nur das traute, hochheilige Paar. Holder Knabe im lockigen Haar,
   Schlaf in himmlischer Ruh, Schlaf in himmlischer Ruh!

"Fum, Fum, Fum"

Placidly   Catalonia

1. On De‑cem‑ber twen‑ty fifth sing fum, fum,

fum; On De‑cem‑ber twen‑ty fifth sing fum, fum,

fum. On that day a Child was born, all pink and white at break of

morn, In a sta‑ble dark and drear‑y lay the

Son of Vir‑gin Mar‑y, fum, fum, fum.

2. Christmas is a day of feasting, fum, fum, fum,
Christmas is a day of feasting, fum, fum, fum.
In hot lands and in cold, for young and old, for young and old,
We tell the Christmas story,
Ever singing of its glory, fum, fum, fum.

1. Veinticinco de dicembre, fum, fum, fum.
Veinticinco de dicembre, fum, fum, fum.
Nacido ha por nuestro amor, el Niño Dios, el Niño Dios;
Hoy de la Virgen Maria en esta noche tan fria,
Fum, fum, fum.

"Hava Nagila"

Folk song from Israel

Hava nagila, hava nagila, hava nagila vé nismé cha [repeat]
hava né ra né na, hava né ra né na, hava né ra né na, vé nismé cha [repeat]
Uru uru achim, uru achim bélevsa meach, uru achim bélevsa meach,
uru achim bélevsa meach, uru achim, uru achim bélevsa meach.

Source: Robert W. Winslow and Leon Dallin, *Music Skills for Classroom Teachers*, 7th ed. Copyright © 1988 Wm. C. Brown Publishers, Dubuque, Iowa. All Rights Reserved.

A P P E N D I X · 3

Guitar Chords

E A D G B E

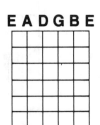 **C**

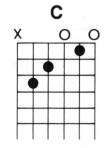 **Cm**

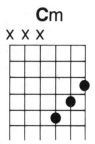 **C₇**

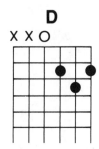 **D**

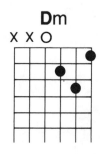 **Dm**

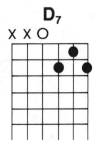 **D₇**

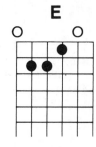 **E**

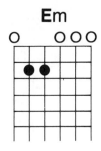 **Em**

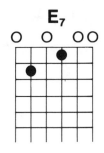 **E₇**

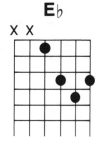 **E♭**

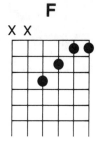 **F**

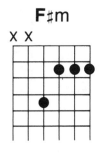 **F♯m**

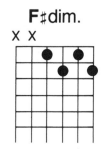 **F♯dim.**

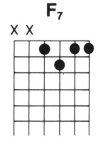 **F₇**

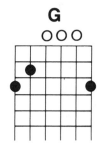 **G**

"O" means open string
"X" means this string is not played

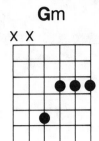

Gm

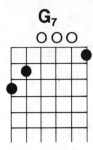

G₇

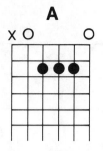

A

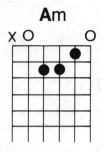

Am

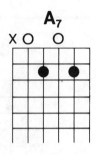

A₇

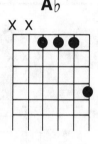

A♭

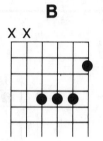

B

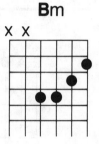

Bm

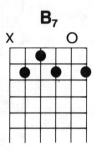

B₇

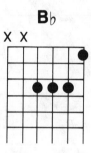

B♭

A P P E N D I X · 4

SOPRANO RECORDER
(Baroque Fingering)

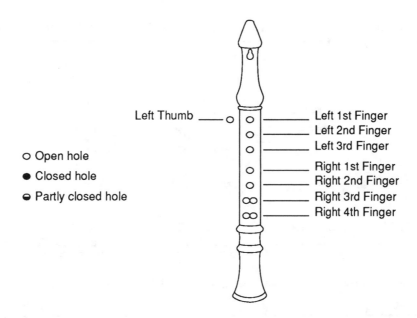

Left Thumb ——— o

o Open hole
● Closed hole
◒ Partly closed hole

Left 1st Finger
Left 2nd Finger
Left 3rd Finger

Right 1st Finger
Right 2nd Finger
Right 3rd Finger
Right 4th Finger

A Suggested Progression for Learning to Play the Soprano Recorder

1. First learn the pitches B, A, and G. You need only the thumb, first, second, and third fingers of the left hand. The thumb of the right hand is used on the back of the instrument for support. The third finger of the right hand may rest on the front *between* holes.

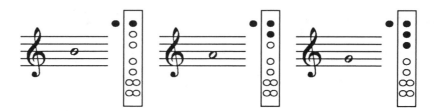

Hot cross buns, hot cross buns,

One a pen-ny, two a pen-ny, hot cross buns.

2. Add the pitches E and D. For these pitches you will use the first, second, and third fingers of the right hand.

Old Mac-Don-ald had a farm, E - I - E - I - O. And

on this farm he had some chicks, E - I - E - I - O. With a
(cows)
(pigs)

Chick chick here and a chick chick there here a chick there a chick, Ev' ry where a chick chick

Old Mac-Don-ald had a farm, E - I - E - I - O.

3. Add the pitches F and C. The fourth finger of the right hand will be added for these pitches.

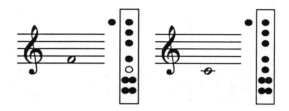

4. A song using these pitches is "Michael Row the Boat Ashore," page 227.
5. Add C: 8. Add F# (G♭):

"On Top of Old Smoky," page 224.   "Alleluia," page 221.
"Sweet Betsy from Pike," page 229.   "Simple Gifts," page 234.

6. Add D: 9. Add B♭ (A#):

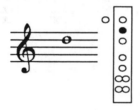

"Morning Has Broken," page 223.   "Streets of Laredo," page 221.
"The Sally Gardens," page 227.   "Dona Nobis Pacem," page 232.
"Wondrous Love," page 236.   "All Through the Night," page 233.
"Scarborough Fair," page 190.   "Red River Valley," page 189.
                                   "Aura Lee," page 182.
                                   "Go Tell Aunt Rhody," page 171.

7. Add E: 10. Add G# (A♭):

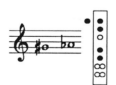

"Love Somebody," page 231.   "Fum, Fum, Fum," page 238.
"The Tailor and the Mouse," page 235.

11. Add F: 12. Add C♯ (D♭):

"Silent Night," page 237.   "Sakura," page 180.

Remaining pitches:

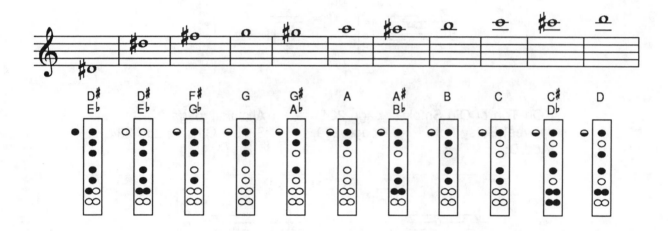

GLOSSARY

accidentals   sharps, double sharps, flats, double flats, and naturals, when introduced apart from the key signature

altered chords   chords that remain in the key of the composition but contain raised or lowered tones

anacrusis   a fractional measure, containing only a single beat or a fraction of one, preceding a complete measure; upbeat; or pickup

answer phrase   the second phrase in a period, or musical sentence

anticipation   a chord tone that advances to the next chord ahead of the chord tones; the reverse of suspension

asymmetrical meter   a musical composition meter in which dissimilar simple meters are combined

bass staff   the lowest set of parallel lines in the great staff

beam   a line connecting two or more notes of values less than a quarter note

beat   the rhythmic pulse in music

cadence   in harmony, a progression of chords that brings the music to a point of repose

chord   the simultaneous sounding of two or more harmonic intervals

chromatic interval   the alteration of the upper or lower tone of an interval by the addition of an accidental, or accidentals, so that it is no longer in the major scale

chromatic scale   a scale in which the tones are a half step apart

chromatic sign   a sharp, double sharp, flat, or double flat

clef sign   the symbol, placed in a specific position on the staff, designating the names of the tones placed on that staff

common time   in modern usage synonymous with $\frac{4}{4}$ meter

compound interval   an interval of more than one octave

compound meter   a musical composition meter in which each beat of each measure is divisible by three

consonance   blending sounds, or sounds in agreement

contra octave   the octave immediately below the great octave

cut time alla breve (It.), in modern usage synonymous with $\frac{2}{2}$ meter

da capo (D.C.) an indication to repeat from the beginning of a musical composition

dal segno (D.S.) an indication to repeat from the sign ℅

deceptive cadence in harmony, the progression from the V to vi chord

diatonic interval an interval that has an upper tone that falls in the major scale of the lower tone

diatonic scale a scale consisting of a mixture of half steps and whole steps

dissonance incomplete or unresolved sounds, often possessing a conflicting quality

dominant the name given to the fifth tone of a major scale

dotted note a dot placed to the right of a note prolongs the duration of the note by half its value

double bar two vertical lines at the end of the staff indicating the conclusion of the composition, or of a musical unit complete in itself; two vertical lines in the middle of a composition indicating a time change, key change, or separation between verse and chorus

double flat the pitch of an individual note already flatted in the key signature may be lowered another half step by the use of a double flat sign (♭♭)

double sharp the pitch of an individual note already sharped in the key signature may be raised another half step by the use of a double sharp sign (♯♯)

doubling the use of one tone twice in four-voice harmonization

duple meter a meter of music in which each measure contains one strong pulse and one weak pulse

duplet two notes that sound in the time of three notes of the same value

enharmonic two different letter names that refer to the same pitch

fermata a pause mark placed over or under a note or rest (⌒); indicates that the note or rest is to be held longer than its normal duration

figured bass a system of labeling chords with numerical designations, used in the baroque era; the numbers indicate the chords to be used by the performer

fine a word that marks the end of a musical composition

flag a symbol attached to the note stem to designate a value of less than a quarter note

flat a sign placed before a tone to indicate the lowering of the pitch by one half step (♭)

form the structure or pattern of a musical composition

F staff bass staff; designated by the symbol 𝄢

great octave the octave immediately below the small octave

great staff eleven lines, the center one implied, on which musical symbols are placed

G staff treble staff; designated by the symbol 𝄞

half note a note half the value or duration of the whole note

half rest a short thick line or horizontal bar that sits on the third line of the staff to indicate silence

248

harmonic interval two different tones sounded together

harmonic minor scale a relative minor of any major scale, using the same key signature, and with the addition of a sharp sign to raise the seventh tone; also referred to as "modern" minor

harmonization the process of adjusting effective chords to the basic tones of a melody

harmony the science of chord construction and progression

hemiola a deliberate shift in the rhythm of a musical composition from three pulse to two pulse or from two pulse to three pulse

interval the difference in pitch between two tones, or the distance between two pitches

intonation the degree of adherence to a correct pitch; playing or singing "in tune"

irregular rhythm the falling of the shorter notes in a measure on the strong pulse

leading tone the name given to the seventh tone of a major scale

ledger (leger) lines short lines used to extend the upper and lower ranges of the staff

major scale the most common type of scale, consisting of eight tones separated by whole steps between one and two, two and three, four and five, five and six, six and seven; half steps occur between three and four, seven and eight

measure groups of tones separated from each other by vertical lines on the music staff, rhythmically grouped in accented and unaccented beats

mediant the name given to the third tone of a major scale

melodic contour design or shape of the melodic line

melodic interval two different tones sounded consecutively

melodic minor scale a relative minor of any major scale, using the same key signature; the ascending scale raises the second and third, the sixth and seventh steps; the descending scale is a natural minor scale; also referred to as "ancient minor"

melody a series of tones sounded in rhythm or as a musical line on the staff

meter the grouping of pulses (or beats), within a measure of music, into patterns of strong and weak beats

middle C the tone placed on the implied line of the great staff

minor scale a scale consisting of eight tones separated by whole steps between one and two, three and four, four and five, six and seven, seven and eight; half steps occur between two and three, five and six

mode the difference in the third step between major and minor scales; an arrangement of the eight steps of the diatonic scale in a fixed pattern, commonly in use prior to the seventeenth century

modulation the process of changing keys during a composition

motive the smallest unit of tones possessing individuality in a melody

natural minor scale the relative minor of any major scale, beginning a minor third lower and using the same key signature, with no added accidentals

natural sign a sign used to cancel a sharp or flat sign (♮)

note the symbol used to express pitch and its duration

note head   a symbol, without a stem, used to specify pitch and duration on the staff

octave   the distance between any given tone and the one produced by a vibration twice that speed; if the half step is the smallest recognized difference between two tones, octaves can be divided into thirteen tones equidistant in pitch

passing tones   tones that bridge two chord tones and add interest to the melody

pentatonic scale   a five tone scale with whole steps between one and two, two and three, four and five, and one and a half steps between three and four; this scale may be formed by playing the black keys of the piano in consecutive order

perfect cadence   in harmony, the progression from the V to the I chord or from the IV to the V to the I chord; usually terminates a phrase or composition

period   a complete musical sentence

phrase   part of a musical sentence, usually two to four measures in length

pickup   see *anacrusis*

pitch   the highness or lowness of sound

plagal cadence   in harmony, the progression from the IV to the I chord; often closes hymns ending with "Amen"

prime octave   the note designation of the successive tones from middle C to the octave above

quadruple meter   a meter of music in which each measure contains one strong pulse and three weaker pulses; the third pulse is slightly stronger than the second and fourth pulses

quarter note   a note one quarter the value of the whole note

question phrase   the first phrase in a period, or musical sentence

regular rhythm   the occurrence of the longer notes in a measure on the strong pulse

relative minor scale   minor scales use the same key signature as major scales; therefore, they are referred to as relatives

resolution   in harmonization, the process of bringing musical satisfaction by the logical progression to a chord of consonant character

rest   a symbol used for duration of silence

rhythm   the pulse and duration of sound

rhythmic unit   the note value of the beat in a measure of a musical composition

root   the name given to the bottom tone of a triad

scale   an ascending or descending series of tones arranged in definite order within an octave

sharp   a sign used to raise the pitch of a tone one half step (♯)

simple interval   an interval of an octave or less

simple meter   a musical composition meter in which each beat of each measure is divisible by two

slur   a curved line connecting different pitches of continuous sound

small octave   the successive octave tones immediately below the prime octave

250

staff   a series of parallel lines on which musical symbols are placed

staff notation   the system for showing pitch and duration of notes, or writing music

stem   a vertical line attached to the note head

subcontra octave   the octave immediately below the contra octave

subdominant   the name given to the fourth tone of a major scale

submediant   the name given to the sixth tone of a major scale

supertonic   the name given to the second tone of a major scale

suspension   a chord tone that is delayed in its progression to the next chord, creating dissonance

syncopation   in a measure, the changing of the rhythm so that usually weak beats become strong beats

tempo   rate of speed of a musical composition

tertian   every alternate tone

tertian alphabet   beginning on any letter of the musical alphabet and building up or down by thirds; basic to the study of harmony

tie   a curved line connecting two or more notes indicating continuous sound for the combined duration of the connected notes

timbre   the distinctive quality of sound

time   see *meter*

time signature   two numbers that appear, in a piece of music, as a simple arithmetical fraction at the beginning of the first measure, indicating the time or content of each measure

tonality   an organization of tones and chords in a musical composition that has a keynote around which the entire piece is built

tone   specific musical sound

tonic   the first (and last) tone of a scale

transposition   the performance of music in keys other than the key in which the music is written

treble staff   the highest set of parallel lines in the great staff

triad   a chord composed of three tones, each a third apart

triple meter   a meter of music in which each measure contains one strong pulse and two weaker pulses

triplet   three notes sounded in the time of two notes of the same value

uniform rhythm   uniform distribution of the note values in a measure among the beats or pulses

unison interval   two tones sounded on the same pitch

upbeat   see *anacrusis*

whole note   the note of longest duration in common usage

S O N G · I N D E X

I N D E X

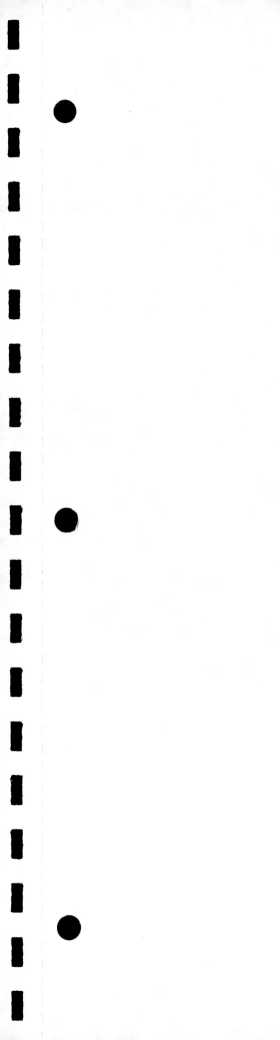

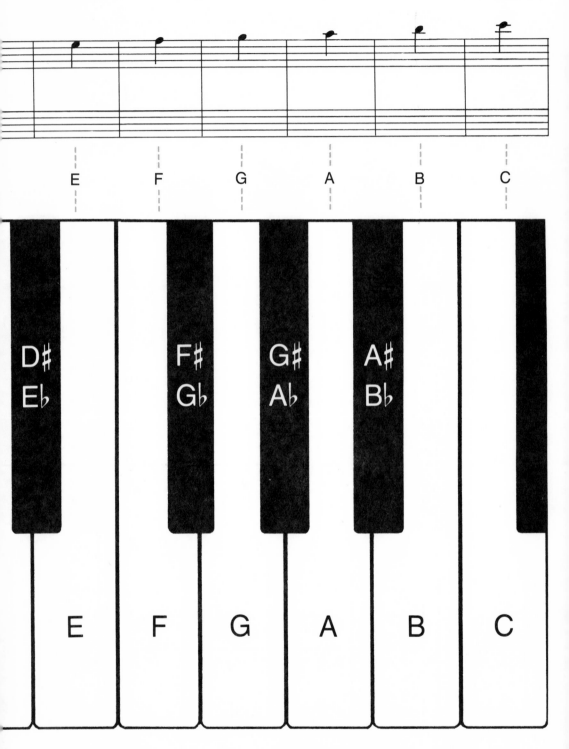

Wm. C. Brown Publishers
2460 Kerper Boulevard   P.O. Box 539
Dubuque, Iowa 52001

and Staff

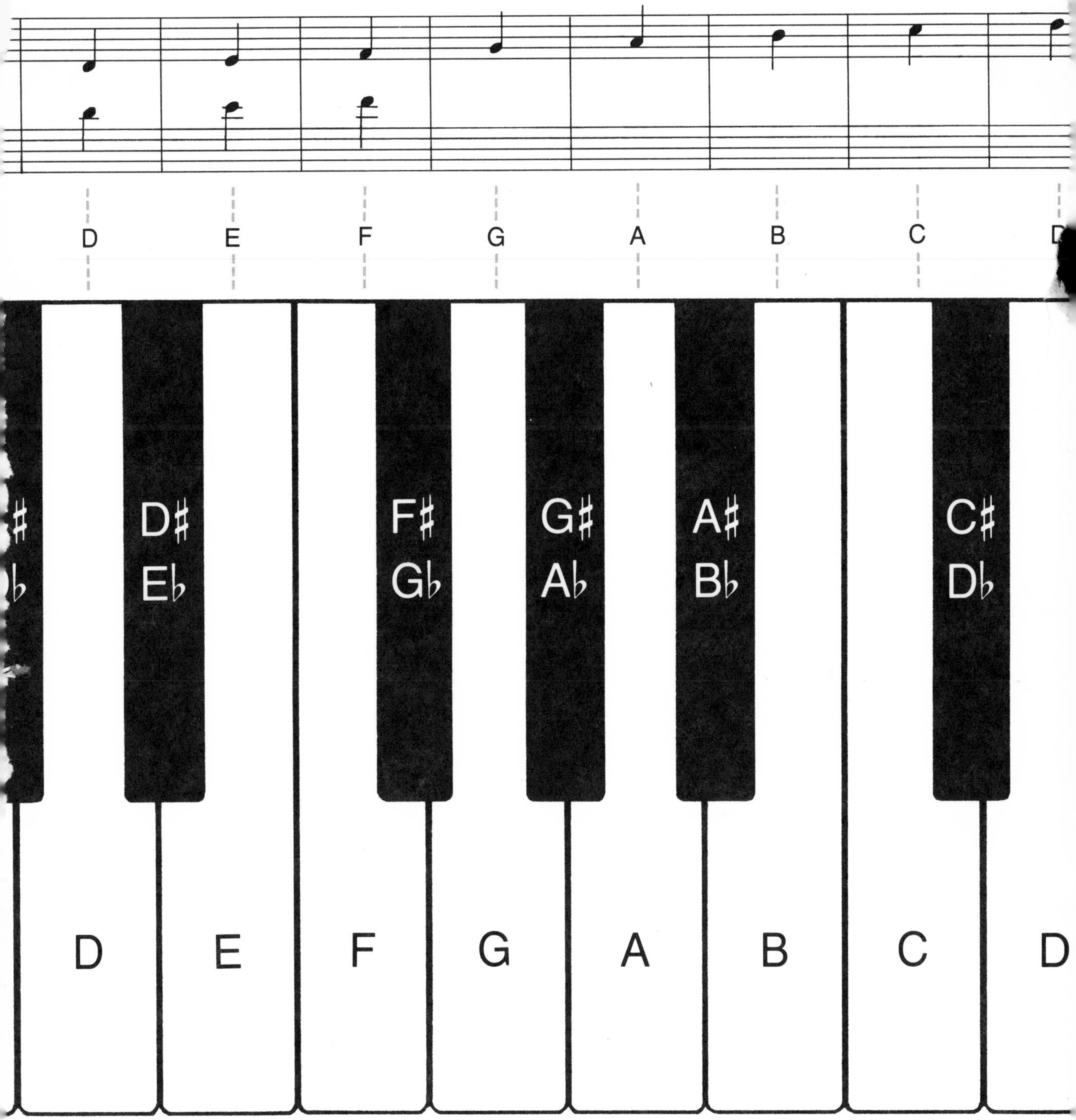

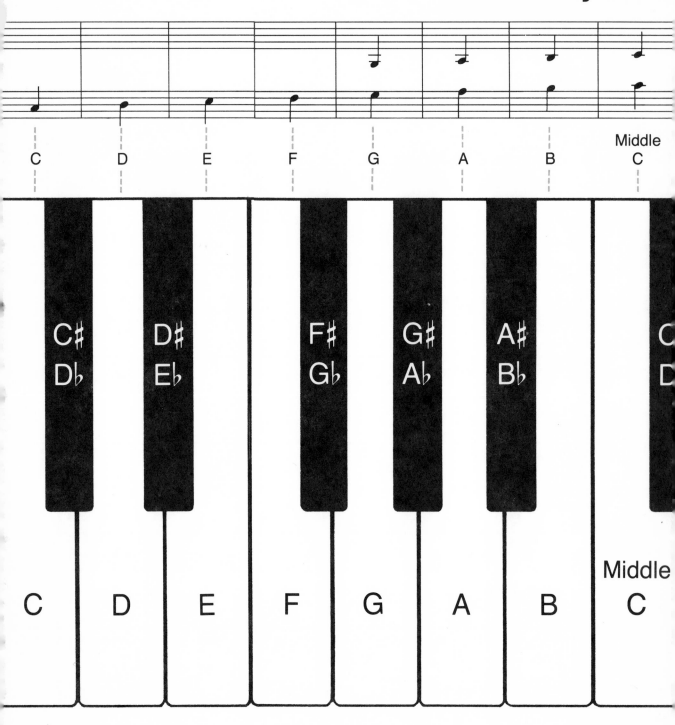

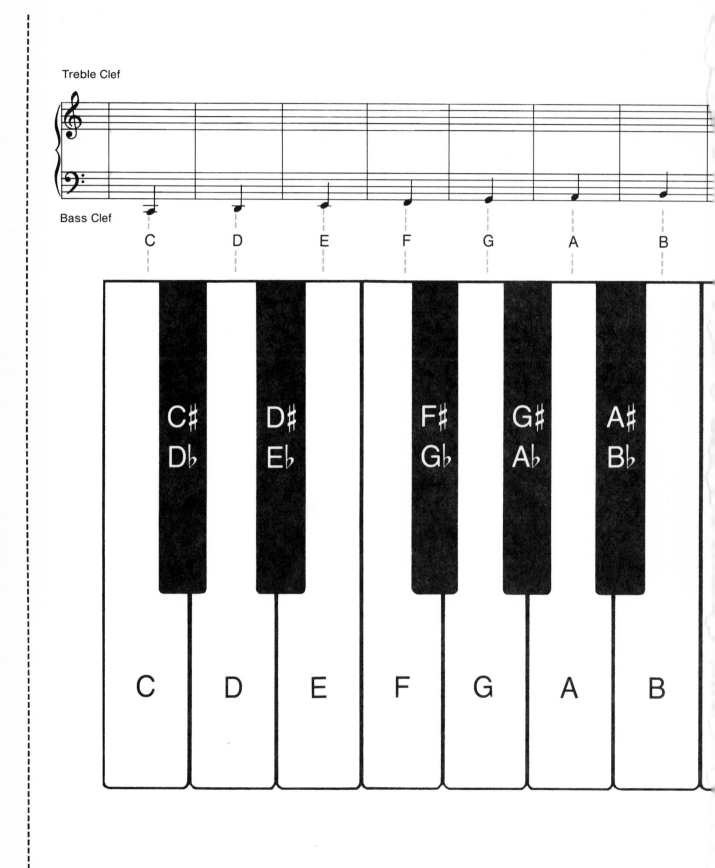